Easing the Ache

Easing the Ache

GAY MEN RECOVERING FROM

COMPULSIVE BEHAVIORS

GUY KETTELHACK

HAZELDEN®

Hazelden
Center City, Minnesota 55012-0176
1-800-328-0094
1-612-257-1331 (fax)
http://www.hazelden.org

Library of Congress Cataloging-in-Publication Data
Crawford, David, 1951–
    Easing the ache : gay men recovering from compulsive behaviors /
Guy Kettelhack .
        p.   cm.
    Originally published: New York : Dutton, 1990.
    Includes bibliographical references (p.).
    ISBN 1-56838-235-9
        1. Compulsive behavior—Case studies. 2. Gay men—Mental
health—Case studies. 3. Gay men—United States—Case studies. 1.
Title.
    RC533.C73   1998
    616.85'84'086642—dc21   97-52185
                                                                      CIP

02   02   00   99   98   6   5   4   3   2   1

Cover design by David Spohn
Text design by Nora Koch/Gravel Pit Publications

Editor's note:
Hazelden offers a variety of information on chemical dependency and
related areas. Our publications do not necessarily represent Hazelden's
programs, nor do they officially speak for any Twelve Step organization.

    Grateful acknowledgment is given for permission to quote from
"Stripping Down to the Id" by David Crawford, which appeared in Issue
260 of *The New York Native*. Reprinted by permission of That New Magazine,
Inc.

For Richard Bell

CONTENTS

Three Questions I'd Be Asking If I Were You

This is a book about the remarkable journeys numerous gay men are taking in their recovery from compulsive behavior. You don't have to know anything about Twelve Step programs to appreciate the journeys you'll read about here, but more than likely you've already heard of, or perhaps even experienced, something of the help the Twelve Step model offers to people suffering from compulsive behavior. If so, you know it's an astoundingly effective and humane program that was first advanced by Alcoholics Anonymous and has now been adopted by numerous other groups that have been formed to help their members recover from various addictions other than alcohol—from drugs and food to sex, work, and unhealthy relationships.

Easing the Ache is in no way meant to be an exegesis of the steps that form the core of this program, but it *is* written in the spirit of Twelve Step recovery. Whatever you know about this process, you probably have a few questions about the book's aims and limits (and, if you do know something about Twelve Step recovery, how closely it's geared to Twelve Step traditions). Certainly my editor had these questions, as did friends who knew I was embarking on this book. So let's address them right off, starting with what may be the first one to occur to you:

WHY A BOOK FOR GAY MEN?

Gay men sorely need a book of their own—this was clear to me when I got the idea for *Easing the Ache,* and it's become clearer now that I've crossed the country gathering material for it. Many gay men feel uncomfortable in "straight" Twelve Step meetings because they don't feel they can share all the "sordid" (and explicitly gay) details of their pasts—or even their present lives. It's not that every Twelve Step meeting isn't helpful—and it's not that gay men don't or shouldn't go to any meeting they want to attend and share whatever they have to share—but there's still a "discomfort level" that many of us admit we feel when we are in "straight" meetings. Some of this uncomfortable feeling extends to our response to "standard" Twelve Step literature too. Much as we depend on it, enjoy it, and continue to be helped by it, many of us get a little weary of having to continually "translate" so much material into terms that more precisely reflect our own lives.

Nearly one out of three gay men is an alcoholic, and we're at least privately aware that we tend to be compulsively "hooked" in many other ways. We've flocked to so many therapies and programs; we constitute a major segment of the self-help book-buying market—and yet, until now, no such book has focused its attention solely on us. We need a book that speaks our language, and *Easing the Ache* is an attempt to meet that need. It is not meant to *replace* any of the literature that's helped us and continues to help us— merely to *add* something vital to that literature: a book about recovery to which we can wholly relate.

WHERE DOES THE MATERIAL IN THIS BOOK COME FROM?

The stories of hundreds of men have fueled *Easing the Ache.*

I've based the book on what I've heard from recovering compulsive gay men in New York, Fire Island, Philadelphia, Boston, San Francisco, Pasadena, Los Angeles, and London. Their widely various experiences and opinions are the stuff of which *Easing the Ache* is made.

If you're familiar with Twelve Step traditions, you know how important anonymity is to the Twelve Step concept of recovery. There is no aspect of this book that has preoccupied me more than protecting the anonymity of the men whose stories have helped form this book. I have gone to the greatest pains to change names, descriptions, and details—there's not one story in the book that is not a complex amalgam of various traits and experiences I've witnessed. I hope the result is that you'll identify with the men you read about here. While every story has been intricately constructed from many parts, every one of those parts is true—but I'm completely confident that no one man's life will be recognizable. If I had any doubts about this at all, I wouldn't have written the book.

WHAT CAN I GET FROM THIS BOOK THAT I CAN'T GET FROM
TWELVE STEP MEETINGS—OR FROM THE STEPS THEMSELVES?

While it's been my experience, and the experience of my recovering friends, that help comes first and foremost from following suggestions in the Twelve Steps and regularly attending Twelve Step meetings, it's also clear that—once you've made the all-important decision to start on the journey of recovery—help is available from many additional quarters. And there's no reason not to reach for as much of that help as you can find.

Easing the Ache is part of that "help." Certainly if you don't have access to gay meetings, one of this book's aims is to give you a potent, distilled "dose" of the "experience, strength, and hope" to be found at those meetings. But even if you do go to gay meetings, I hope *Easing the Ache* will help you dig a little deeper into some of the issues you go to gay meetings to explore. This is a book meant to give us the space to think about our pain and breakthroughs and the safety to face our most shameful and terrifying secrets. It provides an opportunity to explore the special nature of recovery as you and I experience it.

While you won't find the Steps recounted here in their bare form (other books provide "official"—and wonderful—explanations of the Steps; you'll find them listed in the resources section of this book), you *will* get a sense of what it's like for gay men to face and triumph over cropping self-views—what it's like for a gay man to live according to Twelve Step principles. So many people tend to be intimidated by their first exposure to the Twelve Steps—they can seem like such a lot to accomplish! I've made no attempt to cram them down anyone's throat. As I've said, you don't have to know anything about Twelve Step recovery to appreciate what you'll find in this book. Whether you're already "working" the Steps or not, I hope *Easing the Ache* will simply be a good companion—a "gay friend" who might help you think a little more deeply about what it means to *be* gay and "recovering."

The lives of recovering compulsive gay men are adventures—and the bottom line is that we have some amazing stories to tell. I've found it immensely healing to focus on what we have to say. I hope you will, too.

Chapter One
Premise: Hell Has an Exit

What gave birth to this book?

As a recovering alcoholic, I know that my sobriety is a gift—one that continues to grow with all the nurturing I learn how to bring to it, as long as I practice the principles of recovery that other alcoholics have discovered work to keep them sober. One of my first and biggest revelations was that so little was to be gained from the exercise of unaided will. Boy, was this news! All that white-knuckled, constipated straining to control things—people, work, my own feelings and behavior—all the *effort* I'd been taught to expend by the American work ethic and various Victorian notions of progress, filtered through parental admonitions and my fourth-grade teacher, none of that really works. I could not stop drinking through any will of my own. I have since learned that I can't do much of anything else without help either. It's a great humbling truth, and it has saved my life.

Sobriety floods in when I allow it to flood in. My recovery has depended on an ongoing process of surrender, acknowledging my powerlessness not only over alcohol but over most of what fate decides to visit upon me. This doesn't turn me into a doormat. It has the effect of opening my eyes to what's manageable and what isn't. My gratitude for that growing clarity knows no bounds. It's a healing gratitude—thankfulness for the miracle that a terrible compulsion, which once ruled my life, has been lifted. If this sounds as if I've been helped by Alcoholics Anonymous, it should. I have been.

I am also a gay man. Wonderful as my experience of recovery has been, through the same process practiced by millions of other recovering alcoholics in AA, my sexuality did turn out to be a pea under the mattress—a nagging pain that something wasn't getting addressed as directly as it needed to be.

The problem was partially one of translation. Both in AA literature and at the meetings there were so many heterosexual businessmen with wives and kids, so many people who could relate completely to the television sitcom *Cheers*. They were people whose feelings I have always, ultimately, been able to identify with as a recovering alcoholic, but whose lives were so different from mine that I often found it difficult not to feel separate. Then there were the syntactical snafus I felt pressured to contrive: I didn't feel comfortable saying "he" and "his" and "my ex-lover Richard." My tongue tied itself (sometimes hilariously) into a lot of "I can't understand why This Person . . ." or "This Person with whom I live . . . ," etc. Isolation, to any alcoholic, is a killer, and something was increasing the sense of isolation I felt at predominantly straight meetings. I had to do something about it.

What I did was to start going to gay meetings. Because I live in Manhattan, such meetings fortunately were not difficult to find. I found some astonishing and welcome differences. First, a tone and wit with which I felt comfortable. The gay bar cutthroat bitchiness had drained away, but the easy allusions, the shared experience of sex and Sondheim lyrics and

Fire Island, and tales of debauchery and renewal you had to be there to appreciate: all of this was riveting to me. Sometimes comforting, sometimes disturbing (because facing my self-hate means facing my own internalized homophobia), the meetings were right on the mark. I was where I needed to be.

There was also in gay meetings a special experience of what it meant to be duplicitous. We've all hidden behind so many facades for so long that we don't miss a trick—we are master change artists, usually in a desperate attempt to cover up what we feel are our hopelessly inadequate "true" selves. Recovery from compulsive behavior is vividly a problem of building, usually by the smallest increments, self-esteem—self-esteem that had been crushed in us not only because of the degradation we had suffered as alcoholics but also because we were gay. However unopposed we now felt ourselves to be in the liberal, urban u.s.a., we each had had the private experience, at crucially impressionable points in our lives, of feeling irremediably "different"—and worse. Bad. Sick. Immoral. Worthless.

There was a rich vein to be mined here, and my recovery has, more and more, grown to depend on digging into it. A part of this richness has been another ongoing realization, one that I hadn't heard expressed with the same emphasis anywhere else: compulsive behaviors all have a common root. Nowhere was it more clear than in gay meetings that the reasons for drinking excessively were connected to the reasons that so many of us had anonymous sex obsessively. (It's interesting to me when straight recovering alcoholic friends of mine can't understand why gay sex addicts exist in the age of AIDS—as if this addiction were something less powerful than their own alcoholism.) These reasons were also why we overrated or underrated ourselves, worked ourselves

7

into ulcers, and acted out in any number of other destructive, compulsive ways.

Put simply, compulsions are like bumps in a rug: push one down here and it will pop up there. This is particularly unnerving, not to say terrifying, to me as an alcoholic. I frankly expected all of my compulsive behavior to lift when the urge to drink did—now that I wasn't blotto on a regular basis, didn't I have a shot at being Best Little Boy in the World? However, inescapably, even in the new clarity of not being drunk all the time, I began to watch myself (allegedly clear-eyed) still in the grip of sex and food and work compulsions. They hadn't gone away with the booze, and "willpower" didn't work on them any better than it had on alcohol.

This shared root of compulsive behaviors wasn't something merely acknowledged by the recovering gay men knew: most of them were also working hard to face and change their behavior. Attending and, where necessary, creating groups, generally on the Twelve Step model, they banded together to admit their powerlessness over sexual compulsions, eating disorders, obsessiveness in relationships, and other manifestations of self-hatred that they had too long hidden or denied.

Something astonishing was going on. Something, moreover, I needed to learn about to aid my own recovery. The aim was not only to battle compulsion but also to become fully, joyfully, freely *human*. Gay people, banding and bonding together in small groups, were beginning to define goals that would have been unthinkable to them—and to so many preceding generations of gay men, probably back to classical Athens—before.

I am not an expert at any of this. I am a wide-eyed, eager

observer of a phenomenon I am surprised hasn't been reported before and that I find too exciting not to share. Because I could find no book that conveyed the excitement of broad-based recovery in terms that made full sense to me as a gay man, the idea grew that I should record what I was witnessing. I didn't want Sunday school pap or a censorious political stance that made "gay" seem like a badge on a uniform. I wanted to collect something of the heat—the stumbling, the pain, the revelation, the humor, and the *rawness* of dealing with the compulsive behavior I saw in the gay men around me. I wanted to show the anger, agony, laughter, and, ultimately, the serenity—a spirituality made somehow the more believable because of its utterly untoward origins. Men who once crawled naked through the Mine Shaft were now talking about their sense of God. This was exciting.

Easing the Ache is not meant to replace any other form of therapy or to provide an alternative to Twelve Step meetings. While its spirit overwhelmingly derives from the Twelve Step approach, and the meetings that generate the recovery it chronicles, it's not a gay Big Book or a gay gloss on what Steps Three, Five, and Eight mean. Other books, some with the official imprimatur of AA, exist to do that already, and they're better at it than I ever could be. (See the resource section.)

What I hope *Easing the Ache* will be is a book on recovering from compulsive behavior to which gay men can readily relate. What I *know* it is, is a testament to gay men who, despite track records of addiction that are appallingly worse than those of nearly every other single group, are confronting their own self-destruction and finding ways to halt it. They also seem to be creating, unwittingly, a model of recovery from more than booze, sex, drug, or food addictions. By getting down to the bones of their disease, by lifting up the rug to see what "animal" underneath is causing the bumps, they are learning to release themselves from bonds that have stunted the growth of every human being who has ever undergone the hell of self-hatred: they are showing us all how to be human.

No book can substitute for the private recognition of having reached your own dead end, a recognition that seems to be a universal prerequisite for recovery from compulsion. *Easing the Ache* makes no grandiose claims: it won't *make* anybody stop drinking, smoking, having dangerous anonymous sex, or overdosing on drugs or food. But if you've glimpsed to any degree that your own behavior is trapping you—if the thought "there must be something better than this" has ever occurred to you—*Easing the Ache* will show you what numerous other gay men have experienced that "something" to be. Whatever the degree or nature of your own self-destructive behavior, you should find a lot to identify with here. And much, perhaps, to help you heal.

Why are so many gay men fascinated by the topic of compulsivity? Why, when I mention the idea of this book to friends who know nothing more about the Twelve Steps than that they have something to do with the Betty Ford Clinic, do so many pupils dilate? Some tentative answers are emerging for me—you'll undoubtedly be able to speculate from your own experience and add to or clarify what I've found.

Certainly the clearest problem the majority of us appear to face as gay men, whatever the degree of our compulsivity (or ability to acknowledge it), has to do with the rock-bottom issue of self-esteem—a profound self-mistrust that gay people have in addition to what seems to be an epidemic of self-mistrust in the "general" population. The sociology of just about everyone living in Western civilization in the latter part of the twentieth century—but especially the baby boomers—has some pretty bleak aspects. We live in a world so saturated by the media that we've got what amounts to a fun-house mirror relation to the culture: all our rites of passage have been acted out for us on the TV screen—all the rites of passage, that is, that we've been *told* we ought to be undergoing. Certainly this is truest for those of us who were Beaver's age when Beaver was prime-time. Our puberty was ushered in by no less than the Beatles; Woodstock and Stonewall gave us permission to screw like bunnies just when we were at an age to take advantage of it; and now the Golden Girls tell us it's okay to get old as long as we keep up the snappy banter. Any sense of inner self, of growing in any privately earned "spiritual" way, has been swamped.

If this is a general problem of society, and then you add to it the secret, devastating shame most of us felt about being gay, you've got a real recipe for disaster. When most of us discovered that we weren't taking to Little League as we knew Beaver would have, when something deep in us knew that Mr. and Mrs. Cleaver would *not* have been glad to learn that we were lusting after their elder son (Tony Dow in a T-shirt!), our young minds quickly grasped the fact that we weren't the little boys America wanted. Our secret, we felt, made us monstrous.

Then—*whammo*—came 1969.

Suddenly it was not only okay to be gay, we were supposed to be proud of it! We never stopped to reconcile *My Three Sons* with our first three tricks; most of us simply threw ourselves into the "new, improved" sexual fray, grabbing up all we could, reflecting on none of it. It's not that we weren't, on the face of it, delighted with the largesse that was suddenly, unaccountably ours—it's just that something inside us wasn't convinced. Hell, something inside us wasn't even touched. A sense of self we could each, privately, call our own was never really nurtured.

The result is something that neither Ward Cleaver nor Gay Pride ever prepared us for: a terrible feeling of emptiness. The glitz and storm of sexual revolution, Me generations, I'm-okay-you're-okay exhortations all happened outside of us. Nothing seemed to seep in, to touch the place inside that really needed touching, the place where we felt most like our true selves.

But since we've implicitly been taught the answer would come from *outside*—that's where all our other "answers" came from, wasn't it?—many of us continued to keep our antennae up, keep receptive to the next, enticing quick fix. With Madison Avenue's powerful encouragement, we've clung tenaciously to the hope that salvation (or at least relief) would arrive if we bought, drank, used, wore (or had sex with) the right commodity. We've tried to believe that we had only to open the right box, bottle, or zipper.

Gay men certainly aren't the only ones susceptible to the enticement of quick fixes, but—perhaps because of the desperate desire we had to blank out the deeply felt, corrosive certainty that we were "sick"—we *do* seem to have fallen especially hard for the quick-fix line. In fact, *we* were the guys who often made the line so palatable. Gay men have created so much of the music and color and art and style and wit that has fueled movies, Broadway, discos, advertising, and Middle American housewives' dreams. We are an extremely imaginative bunch.

What we've created so imaginatively hasn't, however, only been some of the most exciting and expressive culture in our society—we've also created some ingenious tactics for self-evasion.

There comes a point when the culture (even if you've largely participated in creating it) can't tell you who you are. When Calvin Klein, after all, isn't enough. When Donizetti, Judy Garland, Sondheim, Northern Italian cuisine, Montserrat Caballe, gourmet emporia, San Juan, Paris, Cherry Grove, baths, bars, the bushes of Central, Golden Gate or Griffith parks, cocaine, porno movie houses, Stolichnaya, poppers, Mrs. Fields's chocolate chip cookies, and the latest Merchant-Ivory movie don't cut it anymore. This "point" is more than bewildering. It can be terrifying when you've embraced quick fixes to the degree so many men have, and, suddenly, they don't work anymore.

Our sociology as gay men hurts because it reveals a crippling fact: many of us have never truly learned to *look* at (much less love) ourselves. When rioting drag queens at Stonewall ushered in the Age of Gay, most of us tagged along on the newly opened path to bars, discos, and baths, but not to any deep sense of self-acceptance. We may have "come out," but few of us looked *in*. "Gay" was an adjective, like "hunky" or "stylish" or "sophisticated." Accepting ourselves as human never seemed, somehow, the point—or even especially necessary. Sensual excess was an understandable by-product: accepting the surface of things, we did our best to make that surface satisfy.

For the men in this book—perhaps for you, too—that surface has worn off. The behavior to which we've clung in order to prevent us from looking deeper into ourselves has lost its power to placate, erase, assuage. We've all felt the horror of thinking we were left with nothing.

We've had to face an even less glamorous truth. Whether

it was alcohol or pills or sex or food or work or cocaine, we were gripped by substances we couldn't stop consuming, because we couldn't quit—even though, in many cases, it was clear our lives were being ruined by it. Although we couldn't imagine living differently from the way we always had, we knew something had to give. Life wasn't life anymore. Something had to happen, but who the hell knew what?

Hadn't we squeezed out of the world all it could possibly give us? We'd explored every inch of flesh, mixed and consumed every possible combination of substances, gone everywhere there was to go. There wasn't a speck of uncharted territory out there.

The flash for me—and for the men you'll meet in this book—is that the answer wasn't, after all, "out there." It wasn't in Oz *or* Kansas. It was somewhere so obvious and so accessible that those of us who called ourselves "gratefully recovering compulsives" still wonder at the discovery.

Unfortunately, it often seems you've got to go to hell before you can find this out. One thing my friends and I promise: hell has an exit. And sometimes it can help to hear how others have found that exit, even if you haven't quite yet located your own key.

Chapter Two
The Nature of the Beast

Walk with me, west, down Christopher Street toward the river. It's 9:30, a Wednesday morning in July. The heat is so grimly oppressive it's almost funny. It's like a live presence you have to placate to survive—it changes how you breathe and walk. The day's garb is haze—a pregnant, muggy whiteness indigenous to Manhattan, woolly air that doesn't exist in quite the same form anywhere else. An immense, dank blanket shed by the Atlantic, saturated with the city's own sweat, swallows you. You can taste it—metallic, like nicotine.

The candle and leather and candy shops (which aren't yet open and look, somehow, in this light and at this time of day, as if they never will open again) give way, as we get nearer to the river, to monolithic brick buildings and warehouses converted into co-ops. All their yuppie inhabitants have gone to work.

There is no emptier place than Christopher Street on a hot July weekday morning. It feels especially empty because of its occasional lone wanderers. Come with me down to the end of the street where it butts into the West Side Highway. Take a look at the man on the corner, waiting to cross to the piers that finger the Hudson River. You're about to spend the day with him.

His jeans, which once were white, are heavily stained (you can only partially guess by what) and tight. His genitals form a lump, outlined in sharp relief, from crotch to right thigh. A black spandex tank top girdles his soft upper body. His shoulders, pale and slightly plump, with the odd bluish bruise, escape the wide armholes; his arms are thin and his fidgety hands light a cigarette. Look at his face. His eyelids are puffy, as if they have been recently punched. His eyes are pale and gray, the pupils dull—closed as a warehouse door, empty and dark inside. He does move—his head turns to take you in, eyes recording your form, sizing you up, lingering below your belt. You feel vaguely gutted from his glance, as if it has sucked something out of you. Now he turns back toward the river and the piers—flat peninsulas are dotted on the edges with pale deposits—half-naked men on towels, "sunbathing."

The cars and trucks speed by in front of you. The lanes of the highway seem frantic, in surreal contrast to the hazy emptiness behind you on Christopher Street and beyond toward the Hudson. Finally the traffic light flashes green and you watch the pale man scurry across the lanes. He has to hurry as trucks bear down on him. A disembodied voice yells "Faggot!" (our wanderer doesn't react), the brief spate of green light barely giving him enough time to get across. You have the sense that the traffic wants to crush him into the pavement, like an insect. But he makes it to the other side; the frantic mechanical rush of the highway resumes.

His outline is vaguer now, across the highway, more enveloped by the haze, but you can see his right hand pat down below his belt, rearranging the lump, patting it as if to make sure it's still there or in some halfhearted attempt at arousal. You watch him quicken his pace, climb over a waist-high concrete barrier, over piles of discarded beer cans, weasel his way through a hole in the chain-link fence, and make his way down the side of the first pier. The pale deposits of men in front of him shift and variously open or close their limbs in mute welcome or rejection. But the wanderer moves on. He wants to see the rest of the pier, the rest of the prostrate men, and he'll want to see the next pier after this, more men, more piers. Maybe then he'll drop into a bar for some more "serious" cruising. Some cold vodka would be nice in this heat. He adjusts his belt—he likes either to hike up his pants so his soft middle won't bulge or push them down to hip level so his soft middle won't bulge. He wishes there were a mirror or a car window out here on this pier—something to check out how he looks. He hopes his crotch looks good. An extra film of sweat breaks out as he sees a man walking toward him. His hand flicks down again, reflexively, to check the bulge in his pants. Nice hair on the chest of the man walking up; the guy's a little fat and old, but for some reason our wanderer wants to make sure they cruise each other. The man's eyes travel down to our wanderer's crotch and register disappointment. Shit, the wanderer thinks. Fuck you. A terrible picture flashes through his mind: suddenly he sees himself as sloppily over-weight and soft and ugly and repulsive, pitiably underendowed where it counts. Fuck. Out of long habit, he pushes the picture away, hikes his belt over his belly instead of under, and sucks in his gut.

Our wanderer prides himself on the fact that every part of his body has, at various points in the past, by some man or other, drawn praise. He knows that under the right conditions (in the dark, stretching out at the right angle on a bed), he still can look hot. His belly, he knows, isn't so taut anymore, but he has really nice chest hair. Remember that old queen who'd said he had the nicest chest he'd ever seen? (Of course, the guy was about seventy and drunk out of his gourd.) He wishes he could check himself out in a mirror. His belt chafes his skin, the bulge in his crotch has shrunk, and he feels uncomfortably hot. It would be very nice to have a drink.

He tries to think what would turn him on the most. If he could have anything in the world right now, what would it be? His mind can't conjure anything good enough. He guesses he'd like some guy to go down on him, but even that doesn't register clearly—damn, he hates it when he can't fantasize.

He wishes it were closer to noon so he could have a drink. He knows some bars that are open in the morning, but he doesn't want to seem desperate. Maybe if he had something with grapefruit juice in it. Vitamin C would be good for him, probably. Anyway, people drink this early at brunch on Sundays. Who made the rules about only having brunch on Sunday?

He lights another cigarette and feels his diminished pack. He'll go to the bar on Tenth Street. It is, after all, getting later. How much money does he have? Let's see, $1.75 per drink— they usually give you a free drink every third one, so that's $3.50 for three drinks—plus money for cigarettes. He could get one of those two-for-one deals on some unpopular brand, probably. How much would he then have left? He wanted to have a good long day. He could manage. Maybe, if he had to, he'd pocket a few tips off the bar. Nobody would notice. He'd gotten good at doing that. Also at picking up drinks left by people who went to the men's room. He'd be fine.

He retraces his steps, passing the guy who had snubbed him (fuck you, asshole—you should get something this good!). He climbs over the beer cans and the concrete fence and is then off the pier. He pauses, looks over to the next pier, tries to see if any of the few men on it look hot. Something in his gut draws him to wander over—something else draws him to the bar on Tenth Street. It's a tough decision. The hell with it. Go to the bar.

He notes, a little absently, how often the bottle has been winning over sex lately. Oh well. Swing of the pendulum.

Our wanderer moves back into the inhabited West Village. The chichi restaurants and the neat Greek Revival brick town houses are unnerving. He can't think exactly why. He visualizes, for some reason, a business cocktail party—one he'd been to last October when he'd done what his boss had called some "very creative work" on a particular account. He could still fit into his gray three-piece suit, and he felt like some character from a Noël Coward play. He felt he was playing rich. The party was at a huge apartment on Central Park West. He drank vodka out of Baccarat and had an "intense" discussion with some advertising copywriter he suspected was gay. Someone had taken a picture of him; he liked that picture. He was flushed, gesturing dramatically, brow furrowed as if he were delineating some particularly subtle and profound point. He looked as if he knew what he was talking about. Pulled the wool over their eyes once again, our wanderer thought, seeing himself in this glamorous guise. The world was a joke you had to learn to laugh at, and at the right times.

Something tenses his stomach. Who *are* the few people he sees walk by? They look colorless, undramatic, flat. Don't they have jobs? He still has a job, despite the fact that he loathes it and called in sick today to avoid being there. God, the pettiness of work, the stupid protocol and cross-referencing, his boss getting so goddamned upset over everything. He hates his job so much he can taste it. What *is* he tasting? Damn.

His stomach has backed up again. He'll have to walk slowly now, move very carefully so he won't vomit. He'll will himself to calm down, hold down the rising bile. Not, he knows, that much would come up. His insides would just churn and he'd retch, maybe spit up a little water or coffee, as he does nearly every morning. He'd lean against something, feeling light-headed, feeling that strange searing heat in his head and the freezing sweat on his brow, and then it would pass. It doesn't take Freud to figure out why he wanted to throw up: the thought of his job is enough to make him nauseated. And, okay, so what if the vodka he drank last night *has* upset his stomach? He does taste that acidic, postalcohol stuff that always comes up after he's drunk a fair amount. But he doesn't have a hangover. He never has a hangover. Sure, he threw up fairly regularly, but some people's metabolisms were, he supposed, like that. He was a little "sensitive," that's all.

God knows all his life he'd been called "sensitive."

Fuck "sensitive." Another picture flashes into his mind. He is six years old, walking across some vast lawn somewhere up in New England, on a trip with his parents—a summer vacation. He walks down the hill, his hand in his mother's hand. He is dressed in a little dark blue sailor suit, his mother in a flowing navy-and-white floral skirt and a white peasant blouse. He smells the starch from his white collar and walks as if he, the lawn, and the world were made from spun glass. As if he were on delicate stilts. He smiles sweetly, as he has seen movie actresses do on television. Imagining he's in a movie—his father is crouching way down in front of them with a camera—he tries to pose as he minces down the hill. Suddenly, two rough little whirlwinds of boys, ragged and loud and tumbling through like boulders, run across their path, ram into the sailor suit, and knock our little wanderer off his "stilts." The world spins, the glass shatters, and he can't scream out in pain because the wind's been knocked out of him. But when his breath comes back, he screams all right—a shrill, high-soprano, girlish shriek. He can hear the boys jeering from the woods.

Fuck "sensitive."

There were so many things he would rather not think about.

He doesn't understand why people make such a big *deal* of things, for instance. Like his lover. He really should leave his lover—he knows that. He simply doesn't find him attractive anymore, he can't help it. It isn't that his lover is unattractive, exactly; he is just too familiar. He can't help it that sex is only exciting when it is new. That's just the way sex is. Why can't he go to bed with anybody he wants to? It isn't as if he falls in love with anyone anymore.

He doesn't "love" anyone at all, really. Nobody. Oh, he "likes" his lover enough, he supposes. I mean, they get along all right, as long as he isn't being nagged at for staying out all night. And sometimes they do have sex. Okay, he has to be drunk to get anything out of it, but that's okay—it just reduces his inhibitions and allows him to fantasize a little. He knows his lover likes it when he "dominates" him—makes him "beg" for it. When he's drunk he can get into it. It's like turning his lover into a stranger—a trick. Makes it more exciting.

He doesn't like thinking about this much, either. But he

doesn't have to: he's now at the bar. He can have a drink. Fuck'em if they can't take a joke. Vodka and grapefruit juice. In a mug, please—you know, the large glass beer mug. Yeah, that's it. Not too much ice.

New bartender to break in. Shit. He hopes he'll get that third drink free.

That terrible uneasiness again, the wrench in the stomach.

It feels like guilt. But he has nothing to feel guilty about! He's just trying to live his life the way he wants to live it, that's all! So what if he didn't tell his lover he was taking the day off from work? Jesus. He wondered if he'd check up on him, call his office. Fuck it. Who cared if he did? He just didn't want to be bothered today. He could have a day to himself if he wanted. He could do anything he damned well pleased.

Don't bother me. Leave me alone.

That was what he wanted the most. To be left alone.

People were always so needy. They always wanted you to *do* something. They always had opinions about you. Fucking bunch of moralists.

As the first shock of the vodka wears off, the stomach realigns, becoming receptive. We are past the dangerous part, where we might throw up. Jesus, that was so funny when Patrick, the bartender uptown, gave him a shot of tequila and he responded by tossing his cookies all over the bar! You had to laugh at that one—the look on Patrick's face! Ah, yes, sweet vodka—do your *stuff.*

It's really quite remarkable how at ease he feels, deep down. He really is an extraordinary person. Smart, talented. Damn, he is so glad he's given himself this day! He glances for the twentieth time at his reflection in the mirror above the bar. He looks pretty hot in his tank top. Pretty fucking hot. Very nice day this is. Very nice.

He gets the third drink free—good omen! He leaves before the bartender has a chance to see he hasn't left a tip. He's got more to do today—needs his money, after all.

It's now several hours later. Our wanderer has been to two other bars by now—one catering to a vague category of "leather and western," mostly potbellied men in their forties and fifties. Our wanderer can't imagine why unattractive people just don't simply give up, go home, knit, or overdose on something. The second bar has a piano, little flickering pink lights, and a decidedly more flamboyant clientele. The piano plays the predictable *Mame* and *Hello, Dolly* selections, as well as "Don't Cry for Me Argentina" and "Over the Rainbow." Our wanderer joins in on Garland's anthem. He feels in particularly good voice, as he usually does after several vodka-and-cranberries, to which he's switched because it's now the afternoon. (The dark red of cranberries seems to be an afternoon color.) His vibrato is particularly rich. A bald man with tears in his eyes sings along. Arms outstretched, heads inclined toward each other, they harmonize a major third on the final "I."

This is nice, our wanderer thinks, but I want some sex.

Fuck it. Take a cab. East. East Village. Down-to-earth bar over there. Find a fucking *man.*

He doesn't like it when it starts getting late—it means he'll have to think about going home. He'll have to construct some elaborate story about his day. Fuck it.

He'd go home when he felt like it.

Four hours later he's explaining in a very loud voice that D. H. Lawrence was a completely misunderstood and underrated writer and that if the guy to whom he was now speaking would quit being an asshole and go home and read *Sons and*

Lovers cover to cover this very night, perhaps his obviously inadequate sensibility might benefit from the experience. God, he is smart. His words just flow. The guy he's talking to suddenly, unaccountably, bursts into tears. If we listen closely we can hear him blubber over and over that nobody loves him.

What the fuck's going on here, our wanderer wonders?

Ah. The poor slob. Suddenly the wanderer understands—he shifts into his "warm" mode. He is very good at this. He promises his barmate that he will take care of things—he won't have to worry. He'll always be there for him. Perhaps they can move in together someday. Our wanderer could write a novel—the barmate could have the home and lover he has always wanted. They should really think about it. The wanderer really *is* thinking about it too. Things could be so good, if only he were with someone truly *appreciative.* Our wanderer is really such a warm person.

Everyone has always confided in our wanderer. He has memorized the heartfelt entries in his Class of 1969 high school yearbook. He thinks about that yearbook now while he hugs his tearful barmate—in his mind the handwriting scrawls across a page: "I have never met such a kind, sympathetic, understanding, all-around wonderful guy as you in my whole life," one girl wrote. "You are so easy to talk to and that is fantastic. I know you get tired of playing *Peyton Place* sometimes, and all of our burdens are silly little problems"—it was amazing, really, how much he could remember; he could visualize the page, the blue Bic ink—"but you've helped us all so much. Your talents and your intelligence combined with your understanding shall make you a successful person—loved and admired by many people as you are now."

God, once he fed on that. He fed on all those Bic ink messages like a vampire feeds on blood—until it was all drained away. He read them over and over and over until they blurred before his eyes. Until they didn't mean anything anymore. Until he'd drained them of any possibility of being true.

Because he knew, of course, he was a fraud.

It's late at the East Village bar and the sobbing barmate to whom our wanderer has pledged his undying devotion is gone.

Our wanderer has to face going home. He has no more money. He'd have to borrow from his lover again.

Shit, he was drunk. Even he had to admit he was drunk.

Somehow he gets off the stool and heads for the door.

He flashes, for a moment, on a picture of his parents at their highly polished dining room table, looking at him with disgust.

He feels like shit.

Thank God he never has trouble sleeping. He can't wait to go to sleep.

When he gets home his lover is already asleep. On the couch. Which meant he was mad again. *God,* this is boring, thinks our wanderer. He's mad again because I happened to take a *little* time for myself to have a good time. So what if it's four in the morning? Fuck him. *Not,* God help us, literally. That'll be a cold day in hell.

Our wanderer pulls a pile of dirty laundry out of the closet, lies down fully clothed on the floor, and rests his head on the mass of clothes.

He has no trouble falling asleep.

It's a relief to let him sleep. God knows he needed so much sleep in those days. More than he ever got.

It can't be a surprise for you to hear that "our wanderer" was me. I've tried, anyway, to cull from innumerable incidents in my life as a compulsive gay man the quality of one of my days.

It's the barrenness that strikes me now. The complete inability to tolerate emotion—to see a feeling through from beginning to end. The fear of the world—the reflexive attempt to block out any dissonance, any unpleasantness, any truth. The self-hatred—the certainty I was a "fraud." The smallness, deadness of my world. And, perhaps most vividly, the *sameness* to hundreds of other stories I've since heard. Stories that are completely interchangeable with mine.

Not always in their particulars: the gay man who never drank in public but secretly whacked himself out every night on tuinals and cheap sherry; the gay CEO who took a cab several times a day across town in order to spend twenty minutes masturbating in a porno movie house; the gay broker who became so paranoid from cocaine that he hired a bodyguard to accompany him every morning to work; these and other stories differ from mine in detail. But they are the same too.

The wanderer with whom you just shared a day is a man I sometimes still fear and loathe. Slowly, however, I'm learning to replace that hate with love. Sometimes a fierce love. Sometimes I wish I could, through some *Twilight Zone* machination, return to him just at the moment he starts to cross Christopher Street to the piers and grab his arm, pull him back, take his face in my hands, and shake some life into him. It is unbearably frustrating, sometimes, to watch him go through his motions. The tragedy, if so grand a word can describe the banal waste of his life, isn't that he's dying (although he is) but that he's still alive. As long as he draws on a cigarette, "rearranges" his crotch, stumbles off a barstool, he is, dammit, alive. That's what's so hard to bear—watching him navigate the world as if he were tiny and dead, in full ignorance of a central miracle: *he is alive.*

But this angry love does him and me no good. I need to pull in the reins and take a calmer look. The reason I need to go back to the man I used to be isn't to kick him in the ass. It is to remind myself of who I no longer have to be.

Why make the effort if he's no longer around? If I am no longer that wanderer? Because the wanderer isn't, after all, gone. This is vividly clear when I return to that corner of Christopher Street, which I recently did. He was right there, waiting for me: the light flashed green and he all but pushed me across. He waits for me in front of every bar I pass. He waits for me in every dark cubicle of any remaining bathhouse or backroom sex place. He's in the deli where I no longer choose to buy two pints of Häagen-Dazs coffee ice cream, chocolate fudge topping, and whipped cream; he urges me to change my mind. He continually offers me cigarettes, diet pills, poppers. He offers all the ways he knows of obliterating pain—of numbing out. That pale, soft, dying man is still very much a part of my core.

There seems to be a frightened wanderer in each of us—each of us, anyway, who's rammed into the brick wall of his own self-destruction. Left to his own will, his own fears, projections, assumptions, and fantasies, that wanderer can be counted on to beckon us to whatever safety he knows. Faced with an ache he fears will paralyze him, he's fashioned the keys to a remarkable and bewildering variety of trapdoors—ways to escape that ache. In continual anticipation of pain, fear which he's certain will debilitate him completely if he doesn't take immediate ameliorative action, our wanderer becomes marvelously disciplined. Before long, the trapdoors he opens to get away—to escape any consciousness or possibility of pain—are so well oiled and so much used that he's not even aware he's made the descent. Pavlov's dog has nothing on the wanderer: he is preternaturally quick. *Pfft!* and you're through the door, into the safe, warm, unconscious dark of sex . . . Stolichnaya . . . Valium . . . fantasy . . . memories . . . an ingenious array of ways to black out.

So what's wrong with that?

Actually, nothing—yet. There isn't a problem, anyway, until the fabric of reality unraveled by the wanderer's escape tactics has disintegrated to such an extent that escape is no longer possible. When the trapdoors unhinge and the pain you've barricaded yourself against floods the cellar. When nothing *works* anymore.

Such is the wanderer's temperament, however, that he doesn't *stop* when it doesn't work anymore. He does automatically what he knows how to do; he offers you the same menu, no matter that nothing on it satisfies. You accept that pleasure is no longer possible. You settle for numbness. For an exhausted blankness.

This is the point when orgasm gives you no joy, but you masturbate anyway.

When you can't remember the last time you got a satisfying buzz from a martini, but you're damned if you're going to stop with the eighth one because, who knows, maybe the ninth will do it.

When the *thought* of a cigarette is enough to make you spit up phlegm, but you smoke the last one in the pack and go out to get another pack.

When you spend your last ten bucks on pills you buy in the street without really knowing what they are, and not caring. At least, you hope, they'll make you feel *something*.

When you've got four projects due next week and you find yourself telling your boss, sure, you can do two more.

When you realize you've gotten through the tenth day without eating anything more than three tablespoons of low-fat cottage cheese, half a cucumber, and several bottles of Diet Coke a day, and yet the skin is still slightly thick around your waist, so you decide to cut out the cottage cheese.

When you slice yourself the fourth piece of cheesecake, aware that you stopped really tasting anything by the end of the first piece.

When, in other words, the behavior you've depended on for years to ease the ache doesn't work anymore, but you can't, won't, don't stop doing it anyway.

The appalling truth about the wanderer (appalling because you thought he was *saving* you with his gratification tactics) is that he will bang his head, endlessly, against the same walls until his skull cracks open. Until the traffic bearing down on him as he crosses Christopher Street isn't held back by a traffic light. Keeping himself within crushing distance of a steamroller, he will, quite simply, eventually get steamrolled. The hard truth is that he wants, sooner or later, to destroy himself. And he'll take you with him.

What's astonishing isn't that the wanderer defies all sense and logic to continue on this self-destructive path—that's the least astonishing thing about compulsion (that it continues to compel!). The astonishing thing is that the mess he's battering you into may turn into the greatest gift you could hope for. When the mess gets bad enough, even *you* might notice it.

That can set the stage for miracles.

Chapter Three
Bumps in the Rug: A Tour

The stomach, the groin, and the ego: these are what ruled me. The stomach and groin had fairly simple urgencies, readily felt and responded to; the ego was a bit more subtle. Or, more accurately, *noisy*. Ceaseless chatter, intellectualizing, rationalizing, endless nuanced debates, painful shafts of guilt followed by panicked self-justification, detailed fantasies of the past, and grandiose projections of doom or triumph in the future—this is what once passed for "thought." This was the noise my ego created to keep me from facing what I was deeply, secretly terrified I'd find if the noise ever let up: a worthless fraud.

Not that all was noise and confusion. I was capable of fierce, concentrated clarity—the tunnel-vision type of clarity that comes from compulsion. The pursuit of alcohol, sex, food, or approval allowed me to galvanize myself into a working, seamless, robotic face. The "prize" grew larger and larger until it reached what seemed to be the limits of consciousness. I was a setter riveted to a dead duck. In fact, the only relief I knew how to get from the noise in my head was the relief I got from acting out on my compulsions. Then the world became suddenly simple. I knew what I wanted and I knew how to get it.

Was I unaware of the "damage" I was doing to myself? Not at all. I can't begin to count the number of times I walked to a bar, hailed a cab that would take me to the baths, swallowed diet pills, or tore open a box of Entenmann's chocolate chip cookies with an almost supernaturally clear sense of what I was doing—even the "danger" of it. I watched myself as if the watching part of me weren't involved. I'd split away from whatever it was that was "acting out," that automaton body that seemed to manipulate its limbs independently of my will. I sometimes looked down on the proceedings with very little emotion, rather as I imagine Andy Warhol might have watched orgies in his Factory that he hadn't incited. *Hmm,* look at that. Wonder why they're doing that? Wonder why they can't stop?

That detached numbness was what I often felt, anyway, before I started to feel the intense pain of not being able to escape, before my compulsions stopped working even while I continued to act out on them, before I recognized that my powerlessness over my compulsive behavior was less a matter for abstract observation than a searing rod up the you-know-what.

Recognizing my powerlessness over compulsion really means admitting it, not merely "seeing" that I have no control but accepting that I don't. As the first of the Twelve Steps says, "We admitted we were powerless over alcohol [substitute sex, drugs, food, people, work, or money as appropriate]—that our lives had become unmanageable." We'll get to the "unmanageable" part in a moment, but first, what does "admitted" really mean? Recovering compulsive friends of mine remind me it means to *let in.* It means opening a door to something new, something unfamiliar. It means, to some degree, letting down your guard—enough so you risk seeing something in a different way.

We were given the word "admitted" in this context by a man named Bill Wilson, the well-known co-founder of Alcoholics Anonymous. Evidently Bill codified the Twelve Steps in pretty much their final form in one sitting. (Or—as Nan Robertson lets us know in her thorough examination of Alcoholics Anonymous, *Getting Better*—in one lying-down. Bill, appealingly, never stood when he could sit or sat when he could be horizontal.) That the Steps "voiced" themselves to Bill Wilson with the force of revelation now seems prophetic—they've also hit so many of the rest of us like a lightning bolt too. At least that's how the First Step hit me when the mess I'd gotten myself into had become so horrific that not only couldn't I ignore it, but I also couldn't tolerate the pain of it.

In general, messes do seem to have to get horrific before we pay attention to them, before we can decide that our lives are "unmanageable" as a result. However, you're not alone if the very word "unmanageable" sticks in your craw. You might say, "What do you mean? It's not like I can't get out of bed!" (If that's true.) In fact, those of us who've awakened to the unmanageability of our lives have done so on every rung of the descending ladder. It's especially clear to me from my experience researching this book that gay men are awfully good at maintaining the externals of their lives even when what's happening inside resembles dry rot. *The Picture of Dorian Gray* does not have such resonance for us for nothing. Although many of us find ourselves passed out in the gutter (and there have been, God knows, plenty of us down there), there are many—I would very tentatively speculate more, proportionately, than in the heterosexual population—who've managed to hold on to some semblance of structure and outward respectability. Who've managed to hold on to the job, the apartment, and some network of relationships. Maybe you even continued to *look* good—even while the inner self was being eaten away. Getting to the point where you admit your life is unmanageable must, then, be a matter for you to decide. If you're similar to the majority of us, that decision probably won't be too hard to make, because the revelation that your life is falling apart usually hits you, when it's time to hit you, like a load of concrete. But not everyone gets the message in a flash—sometimes it's just a slow accretion of worse and worse "circumstances," at the end of which you realize you're at the end of the rope. However the realization comes, you'll end up feeling overwhelmed by the pressures compulsive behavior brings to bear, and you'll make an astonishing connection: you'll see that the chaos of your life is tied to your own behavior! You won't be able to blame Fate anymore.

Most compulsive people do everything they can to deny this connection. In fact, denial is our biggest stumbling block. One of my favorite bar conversations when I drank was about how alcoholic *other* people were. "Wasn't he awful last night? (Hey, bartender—gimme another vodka tonic, would you?) He really should try to drink less. . . ."

When the "Aha!" moment comes—that *you're* the guy with the problem, not "him" or "it"—it's really nothing more than breaking through denial. It's the core of every compulsive's first moment of recovery. Whether it comes from a knockout blow or from a long series of Chinese water-torture drips, you ultimately find you can no longer blind yourself to your own behavior. The shit you're sitting in is yours.

To appreciate what it means for gay men to get past denial, it may help to take a closer look at some typical obstacles gay men (consciously or unconsciously) have found or put in front of themselves. Through the experiences of gay men with whose feelings (if not always circumstances) I think you'll identify, we'll take a brief tour of the bumps in the rug—a spectrum of compulsive behaviors, as well as the attitudes that seem inevitably to accompany them.

Matthew's choirboy good looks at thirty-five are, in a sense, appropriate: he *was* a choirboy in his hometown Episcopal church. He remembers, at thirteen, the "aura" he'd felt from the church, an attraction which even made him consider (briefly) entering the ministry. "It's what I've heard from so many other gay men," he says. "The beauty of the ritual, the clarity of what to do next, what to believe, the exaltation of stained glass and noble hymns, and"—he winks—"the *fabulous* vestments." His ability to camp about Anglican drag is relatively recent: his only definition of "camp" back then was the humiliating Boy Scout trips his father made him take. Boy Scout trips where the only thrill was the casual rub while another boy splashed in the lake, the sight of your scoutmaster naked in a makeshift shower, the secretive masturbation you practiced, fantasizing about what it would be like to wrestle Ken or Ronny or Bill.

I made this segue because Matthew did: "I was the best little choirboy in the world—and I tried to be the best little Boy Scout in the world too. I was lousy at sports, but I had a knack for tying knots, and something about the *rules* of being a Scout and earning merit badges was as attractive to me as the ritual of the church on Sundays. The problem," Matthew said, sighing, "was the other stuff. The stuff I had to hide. When I discovered masturbation, it was like suddenly I gave myself entry into a secret, dark world nobody could enter but me. It was years before I realized that anyone else even had an orgasm—I thought it was some freak of nature that only I experienced. No one knew what it was like to live in my fantasies but me. I spent enormous energy playing the best little boy—but it seemed only to fuel the other side, my inner fantasy machine. I began to see it as Yin and Yang. Being 'good' meant I had to balance things out by being 'bad.' In my kid's mind—which persists, when I let it, to about right now—I thought 'good' *entitled* you to be 'bad': the more pluses you stacked up the more minuses you were allowed to stack up too. I was a saint so I could be a devil."

How did he see himself as a devil? "It started with my masturbation fantasies, but I couldn't stop with just imagining them. The big taboo—which means my greatest secret goal—was to bring them to life." Matthew once hid himself in the church after choir practice. "With my heart in my mouth, I crept into the choir loft and took off all my clothes. I felt the most unimaginable freedom—thrill and fear. I knew that what I was doing was somehow the worst thing anybody could imagine, and that's what made me want to do it." Matthew had had a crush on another boy, Larry, in the choir, and his fantasies fixated on him. "I sat in the choir loft, reveling in the feel of the polished wood against my bare butt, and imagined Larry opposite me in the loft. I got a hard-on and I beat off. My climax was something I'd never experienced before—an explosion, like all of me came together and then blasted apart. It was the most complete feeling I'd ever known. The terror of being found in church like this was simply *fuel*—it made me want to do it even more."

Acting on his fantasy was like a drug. "I couldn't believe you could actually live out a fantasy," Matthew said. "It was the most incredible revelation. And it began to escalate—right from that moment—starting the very next day."

Matthew repeated his experience in the church three more times that week, the third time narrowly missing a cleaning lady who opened a creaky door just as he'd zipped up his pants. "If she'd come in five minutes before . . ." It was still exciting but didn't have quite the charge of the first time.

Then Matthew realized something. What was so exciting about the church wasn't only its forbidden nature but also that he could imagine Larry being there too. He started to think of all the places he associated with Larry—gym, algebra class, the school band. All those places began to seem erotic. When the idea hit him that he might be able to sneak into those rooms, and beat off, the decision was already made. "I can't believe my gall even now," Matthew says, rubbing his forehead. "I'd sneak into the algebra classroom after school and unzip and masturbate—listening for footsteps or the turn of the doorknob. I'd do the same thing in the auditorium after band practice. And gym—that was harder, but more exciting. I'd see if I could 'get off' after everyone left the locker room for the field. I'd have an orgasm quickly and then run out, as if I'd been late pulling on my sneakers. The more dangerous the place or situation, the more compelled I felt to masturbate.

"When I was about seventeen, my mother walked into my room just as I was cleaning myself off, like I usually did, with my bathrobe. Just the day before," Matthew said, "I'd overheard my mother saying to my father that she'd found my bathrobe, and she wondered, innocently, if moths were laying eggs in it or something, because it was so stiff." Matthew gave a pained chuckle. "Anyway, she obviously knew what I'd just done, and I can't describe—and I'll never forget—the look of disgust on her face. I felt about two inches tall, as if the room had expanded and she was miles away." Later,

Matthew said, when he "slunk" down to lunch in the kitchen, his mother glared at him furiously and blurted out: "You don't know *anything* about sex!"

"It was such a weird reaction, now that I think of it—although it was absolutely true. I *didn't* know anything about sex. And obviously, with my mother and later my father—whom she must've told, because I got a big lecture that night on 'respecting your body'—anyway, given their reactions, I wasn't going to get any information from them." Matthew withdrew into himself, as if "not knowing anything" were his fault, something he should be ashamed of. "And I *was* ashamed. Not only of being caught masturbating by my mother but also of something deeper. There was something rotten in me, something evil, something I couldn't control. And my mother had discovered the truth—the *real* truth. I was evil. I was a rotten human being. Something decent that was in everybody else had been left out of me."

A pattern was set. Matthew threw himself into his church, school, and scouting activities, working harder than anyone else, getting more awards than anyone else, striving with all his might to be the best little boy in the world . . . and then, inevitably, "giving in" to what he thought of as the devil inside him—the "real" Matthew. He'd sneak away to neighboring towns, to parks, to movie theaters, expose himself and masturbate. He felt, somehow, both validated (for proving to himself what he knew he "really" was) and ashamed. One time he became suicidal. "I nearly threw myself in front of the commuter train I was taking to get to other towns—I still don't know what held me back." There was the part of him he called "a sick pig" and there was the "angelic" boy he otherwise struggled to show the world outside.

This was the pattern that persisted into his thirties, except that he began suffering worse consequences: at twenty-five, he was caught masturbating in a department store's men's room. "Not once, but twice in one day," Matthew adds. "Doing it the second time was more exciting because it was more dangerous." He was booked for public indecency—a charge that was repeated two more times in the same town within the following year and resulted in the loss of his job. "It was a small enough town for the judge to know my boss, whom he finally told about me." Matthew moved, got into more trouble. He was completely in the grip of his compulsion. He had, really, no other life. "Sometimes I went to gay bars, and sometimes went home with other men, but something about the intimacy of actually making love to another human being turned me off. The anonymous thing about beating off in dangerous places was so much more exciting. It consumed me. I found ways to beat off in the strangest places—hotel lounges, airplanes, libraries, even once in a supermarket."

Matthew had no friends and no contacts outside his job. "I still tried to be the best little boy at work, and I went to church on Sundays, often vowing to God that this week I'd change, but my life was more and more disjointed—and the 'good' part of it felt more and more like a sham. It was as if I was out to prove how depraved I was—prove it, day after day, to myself. I remember once, after masturbating in the city park, feeling depleted, not sated the way I used to feel after I did that, and walking down the street toward my home. A crazy woman in ragged clothes, with wild hair and eyes, mumbling to herself, turned around suddenly after I passed her and shouted at me: 'You're an *evil* man!' I felt like sinking into the ground. So it's *that* obvious, I thought. Even a crazy person can see it."

Matthew's experience of compulsion has so many aspects

common to the rest of us. The feeling that there is a struggle between absolute Good and absolute Evil is rampant, as well as the ultimate sense that one is *evil*—somehow lacking in the "decency" that everyone else seems to have. I don't know a compulsive person, and especially a compulsive gay man, who hasn't felt it. We are afflicted by such a heavy dose of shame: its roots seem endless. The very notion of looking for those roots is horrifying. Like Matthew, we'd rather do anything than really face what we're sure is the terrible truth about ourselves. Matthew now realizes that his compulsive masturbation was the most effective means he had of escaping any feeling that might draw him into himself—that threatened to reveal how worthless he felt he was. "The only thing I could depend on," Matthew says, "was my penis. That was the only part of me I could depend on to give me relief. Everything else was frighteningly unpredictable—everything else was unsatisfying, risky, imperfect. I felt totally cut off from people; I felt like only half a person at my job; I felt like a hypocrite in church. The only thing I knew how to do perfectly was masturbate. It was the only way I knew of blocking out how terrible I felt about myself."

What's the source of this deep self-mistrust, this overriding sense of shame? "Who knew?" Matthew says. "I couldn't bear to look at it. I know it had to do with my parents not knowing I was gay—I was ashamed of it. I hadn't come out to anybody, really. I know it's that the only way I could conceive of sex was as something dirty and furtive. I'm sure there are a whole load of other psychological reasons too. But the main thing, when I was acting out, is that I never gave myself time to ask myself these kinds of questions. I had a horror of myself. Why would I want to explore that?"

Matthew gives a definition of "acting out" that seems to

apply to most of the rest of us: "I was not only acting out my fantasy," he explains, "but I was also acting out my feelings—literally acting them *out* of me so I wouldn't have to experience them." The urgency with which Matthew felt he had to do this illuminates another aspect that seems to be common to the rest of us: "Once I imagined a turn-on situation, it was as good as done. I had no choice. I couldn't just think about beating off—the second the thought came into my mind, I had to *do* it." This simultaneity of fantasy and action is just one more way to whisk yourself out of yourself. "I'd do anything not to have to think or feel anything remotely threatening," Matthew says. "But the really frightening thing was that the only tactics I had for closing up finally didn't work so well anymore. I began to feel this terrible gnawing in the pit of my stomach, as if some animal were trying to claw its way out. When I see the movie *Alien* I identify so strongly with the guy John Hurt played, acting normal one minute, writhing in agony the next, and then this monster bursts out of him. That monster kept threatening to burst out of me. It was horrible."

I hate to leave Matthew on the verge of that monster's arrival, but his "Aha!" moment belongs to the next chapter. For now, let's stay with the feelings that led up to that awakening—the trepidation Matthew began to feel when he realized that the only survival tactics he knew were starting to break down. The crucial point about Matthew's particular bump in the rug has to do with what's beneath the sense of "depravity" he felt about his life. What's really going on is *deprivation.* Matthew never allowed himself to have a whole emotion: at the first sign of any feeling, whether happy or sad, scared or angry, an inner alarm would ring and his Shut-Down Procedure would be underway. It was as if having any feeling meant the possibility of Matthew making contact with himself: an intolerable idea—anything but that! Like Matthew, every compulsive human being I know has learned instant ways to escape the terrifying prospect of *being with himself.*

This fierce attachment to what we're convinced is lifesaving compulsive behavior is almost always accompanied by some kind of denial—if not denial that we're doing something to excess ("Everybody does this! I know plenty of people who do it more than I do!"), then denial that it's really harming us ("George Burns drank five martinis a day!") or that we can't stop it any time we want. Matthew says he held on to the notion that his compulsive masturbation was "just a way to relieve tension (and the definition of a victimless crime!)" right up until the end—right up until he couldn't stand the despair his compulsion had brought him to. Obviously, we will cling to something we are convinced is our only salvation; with that logic, we'd be fools not to. Denial isn't hard to understand. But it appears in such a bewildering array of guises that it's worth looking into a little further. Several new bumps in the rug about denial will crop up when you meet Grant—bumps that Grant persisted in ignoring even though he kept tripping over them.

"The rules don't apply to me."

Grant was a self-professed snob. He had very little use for most of humanity. He felt an absolute black-and-white morality about everything and everyone in his life. His judgments about people were as swift, clean, and final as a guillotine: "I'd do one of two things to people—deify them, put them on a pedestal they had no idea I was creating for them, and set them apart not only from the rest of humanity but from me. My few gods were worthy even of my own aspirations." The fact that the gods kept slipping off their pedestals didn't really faze Grant: he would simply rewrite history and quickly forget he had ever deified them in the first place. A new god would quickly ascend, and all else would be blocked out. "People not on a pedestal, who were, after all, in the great majority, made me furious because of their stupidity, their inability to see the truths I saw. Stupid people were unbearable. I happily entertained the Swiftian notion that they should all be shot."

At one point in his life, Grant's absolute morality had to do with what he now calls his "high-fat ideals." "I despised people who talked about losing weight, which it seems nine out of ten Americans can't help doing. This was when I'd decided that if it didn't have real butter, cream, or whole milk—I sounded a little like Vincent Price when he used to do those dairy commercials—if it had passed within hailing distance of anything remotely ersatz or reduced-calorie, I'd have nothing to do with it." Grant, during this period, was, unsurprisingly, fat himself. "I was defiant about it. I wasn't like anybody else—the rules didn't apply to me. I could do what I damned well pleased, and if you didn't like it, I didn't like you." It was likely, of course, that Grant had already decided he didn't like you. Again, the friends in his circle were selected for what he imagined was their abject appreciation of the same things he liked. In his fat period, this meant fat music. Grant was an avid music lover and a purist about what he loved: "The thicker and more romantic, the better. Anything before Brahms was *verboten.* I took aural baths of Bruckner, Wagner, Mahler—turned it up loud, got a lot of threats from the neighbors." Except, it turned out, one. Enter first god on the pedestal.

"A man knocked on my door to ask me who was doing the Mahler Fifth he heard coming from my apartment. He looked down in the most angelic, self-effacing way. 'Of course, it's Bernstein!' he said. 'I was stupid not to have realized.'" He was a slight, bearded man—as different as he could be from the elephant Grant looked like then. "But there was something marvelous about him," Grant said, "I invited him in to listen to more. He was delighted." It turned out that Grant's bearded visitor had a degree in musicology from Juilliard but really wanted to conduct—and he loved the same late Romantic repertory that Grant loved. Quickly ("before the end of that afternoon," says Grant), Grant was head over heels in love. He began spinning fantasies of sharing a cottage in the Alps with his beloved, á la Cosima and Richard Wagner. It would be a little nest to which they'd retreat between the maestro's engagements with the Vienna Philharmonic. Grant's friend was everything he could have hoped for: passionate about the "right" music, intelligent, sensitive—everything but, well, gay. Grant's beloved even turned out to be engaged to a woman. But Grant wouldn't be discouraged. Surely once his beloved saw the kind of utter devotion Grant felt toward him, once he saw the kind of selfless helpmeet Grant could be—surely he'd win the man's love. Love conquered all, didn't it?

When the inevitable happened—the guy got married, as planned—Grant's world shattered. None of it computed: he'd worked out the perfect scenario. How could his beloved have perpetrated such a betrayal? He locked himself into his tiny apartment, turned off the lights, tried to listen to the Bernstein recording of the Mahler Fifth that had been Their

Song, but nothing would ease his pain. He would call up his ex-beloved, say nothing, then slam the phone down. He even sent him a telegram over the phone, forcing some poor, unsuspecting operator to recite the words "DAMN YOU TO HELL (STOP) I'LL NEVER FORGIVE YOU (STOP)." After many days of withdrawal, he finally snatched the Mahler off the turntable and smashed it on the floor. He rummaged around for something—anything—different. He found an old recording of a *Brandenburg Concerto,* played on original instruments, and listened to that.

This led to some sweeping changes.

Grant became a baroque purist, literally, from that moment on. If it wasn't performed on original instruments, he wouldn't listen to it. His food habits changed too. He passed a vegetarian restaurant one day, entered, sat down, and decided he'd eat macrobiotic grains and steamed roots. His lunch led to a new morality: all meat and fat were henceforth excised from his diet. To boost him in his new purification regime—which, he decided, depended on as rapid a weight loss as he could maintain—he bought some over-the-counter diet pills. The extra-strength variety. Not satisfied with the dosage the box recommended, he doubled it. He limited himself to 600 calories a day and stuck to this religiously. Wired to a high state of tension by his double dose of diet pills, his metabolism worked overtime and he went from 230 pounds down to 130 pounds in about ten weeks. He thought he might try for 125. His weight had to be a number that ended in either a five or a zero: anything else was imperfect. He sacked his three friends from his fat era. Then, at the performance of a Bach oratorio in church, he found himself sitting next to a pale, thin young man wearing wire rims, a ringer for Woody Allen. They made the same scathing remarks about the performance. ("What do they think they're singing? Verdi?" "God, it sounds like Renata Tebaldi *in heat*. This is supposed to be baroque music?") Enter second god on the pedestal.

Grant proceeded to fantasize in his old wild, excessive ways about a man who (Grant persisted in telling himself) was *not* as inaccessible as his predecessor had been. Grant's food intake, which was now down to 500 calories a day (when he didn't "fast" to "clear out his system") was somehow *proof* that he was purifying himself for this new perfect man. "My Woody Allen friend began getting concerned about how I looked—I guess I was down to about 125 pounds. I thought this meant he loved me and cared about me. Somehow I associated the success I'd had in losing weight with the success of getting this man to express concern about me. I was making him notice." In fact, Grant's friend was alarmed: Grant was wasting away to nothing. He was physically ill by now—weak, pale, and continually on the verge of passing out. But this simply made Grant feel more like Camille—as if he were "honing" his spirit down to bare essentials, becoming a pure flame, denuded of anything extraneous, as spiritual as Joan of Arc, as unearthly as a Botticelli, as lucid as a Bach partita.

Then Grant's Woody Allen friend met a woman, whom he decided to marry.

Grant was admitted to the hospital a few weeks later. One of his neighbors had called an ambulance when she found him passed out in a corridor of their apartment building. A blood test indicated that he'd consumed nothing but extra-strength Dexatrim "with vitamin C added" for the previous two weeks. He was put on an IV, and when he was restored to consciousness, he woke up angry. He was still utterly convinced that he was inaccessible to any human being he knew—and not subject to any "human" (or nutritional) law. He felt unspeakably superior to the rest of the human race. In fact, he felt he had transcended that imperfect, bumbling mass of species; he was something more evolved, rarefied. He was angry—then, suddenly, out of nowhere, devastated. His grandiose sense of himself toppled like a house of cards, and he was hit by the blinding realization that he was a fool, a piece of shit, a worthless scrap of nothing. A stupid creature who'd had the temerity to think he might wring a little happiness out of life. It was time to pack it in. Get off the planet. There was nothing here for him. He wasn't worthy of taking his next breath.

Grant's recovery is grist for a future mill. As cruel as it seems to leave him here, pendulum swinging wildly into depression, he's taught us so much already that it's time to stop to examine it. Our concern here is his despair, because it's our despair too. Perhaps the most striking aspect of Grant's experience is the last part—that wild swing between grandiosity and self-loathing. Clinging to a self-imposed rigid order of things—his high-fat or fatless food regimes, his all-or-nothing approach to music, his abject adoration of whatever "god" he happened to appoint, his hatred of everybody else, his gravitating toward unavailable men, his setting himself up for inevitable disappointments is painfully familiar to most of us. One thing you hear over and over in Twelve Step meetings, and, it seems, particularly from gay men in those meetings, is the perfectionism we all learned to strive for—whether it's something as obviously compulsive as Grant's determination that his weight should end in a zero or a five, or the more subtle demands we make on ourselves to think, act, or feel "appropriately." For "appropriately" read "perfectly." Most of us seem to be driven with a vengeance to uphold an imposed "right way to do things" and a right way to feel about things. I grew up in a household with the implicit message that there was a "right"—to my young mind, that meant *morally* right and handed-down-from-*God*—way to eat spaghetti, drink coffee, tie a tie, sit at the table, shine your shoes, make your bed, and wash your face. My experience, of course, isn't unique: that's how many parents bring up children. But, for whatever "psychological" reasons, compulsive people like me and Matthew and Grant take to this notion of "right behavior" with a terribly heightened sense of fear: stepping on a crack really *will* break our mother's back. Our addiction is as much to this kind of "perfection" as it is to any substance or behavior.

In Grant's case, this haughty I'm-right-and-you're-wrong stance covered up a deep lack of self-esteem, and our own rigidities tend to cover up the same thing. Later, when he began to recover from his compulsivity, Grant could point to his childhood for the origins of his behavior, and (as we'll see later in chapter 9) although it helped to see that his behavior had "historical" roots, it didn't help him to stop acting out compulsively.

It's appropriate here to say something about the psychology of all this. Isn't what we're hearing about in Matthew's, Grant's, and, for that matter, my life, a matter better directed to a shrink? Wouldn't a healthy dose of "analysis" help? As we'll see later on, analysis can be wonderful, and a certain kind of analysis is crucial to recovery from compulsive behavior. But what most of *us* (gay male compulsives) meant by "analysis" was simply rationalization. We are a very canny group: we can be brilliant about the sources of our sick behavior and spend years on the couch being brilliant to our shrinks, but unless we wake up to the simple fact that we've got to *do* something different to get better, not merely imagine various convoluted alternatives for ourselves, we are trapped. Studying each grain of sand in the pit allows you to get to know the pit awfully well, but it doesn't help you climb out of it.

Other aspects of Grant's experience call out to us. Like Matthew, he fled to the "safety" of his fantasies because they were what he could depend on. Unfortunately for Grant, simply having a fantasy didn't mean the "real world" would follow suit. This was a continual, painful surprise to Grant: since he could envision such a perfect way for everybody to behave, why didn't they just do it? Again, his adherence to rigid systems of his own devising is familiar to all of us: out of the desperate, secret fear that we are "nothing" on our own, we often create elaborate shoulds and should nots, dos and don'ts, an inflexible sense of what's tolerable and what isn't. Since we deeply feel nothing like a reliable self, we're damned if we're not going to construct one. When, inevitably, that self topples, we are devastated; we scramble to shore up another one. One compulsive gay man I know talks about his addiction to lying. He sees, clearly, that it comes from how he felt he had to lie to his mother and father—his father because he felt it was only by constructing elaborate, exciting stories about his day that he could get his attention; his mother because her demands were so high he felt the only way he could please her would be to pretend that he'd gotten an A+ on his every effort. But his compulsion really sprang from the desperate feeling that he was hopelessly inadequate as he was. Lying became a modality: it was how he related not only to other people but also to himself. Grant was no less a liar; he'd simply gotten so "good" at it that he could virtually don a new world view as easily as flipping on a switch. However, what all of this scrambling for some semblance of an acceptable self does, bit by bit, day by day, year after year, is to *reinforce* the central sense of ourselves that made us want to lie in the first place: with every lie we tell ourselves we are worthless.

The ways we try to hide our lack of self-esteem from ourselves are poignant—and virtually infinite! Of course we are going to try to escape our self-hate: who wants to feel self-hate? But our elaborate constructs, the desperate clinging to any behavior that will allow us to continue to believe in the fiction of those constructs, will inevitably topple. We can't hide from ourselves forever. The question is, what do we do when we finally come face-to-face with that horror—the horror of seeing yourself naked and frail and fallible?

I'm most struck by the drama of that particular moment in the following story—dear, gorgeous Peter's story. There's still a part of me, the part of me that's still ego-bound and blind, that can't understand why physically beautiful men have any problems at all. And Peter, perfect as he seemed to be, can give us a great lesson in just what a cover-up that kind of beauty can be.

"Just try to stop me."

In his mid-thirties—tall, dark, mustached, and strikingly handsome—Peter kept his "package" in good shape. He banked on his physical attractiveness and his charm. He came out at twenty-two in San Francisco, where he'd moved right after graduating from a small progressive college in the Midwest. This was San Francisco's gay heyday (the mid-seventies), and Peter, with his good looks, found himself in the center of it. Being in the center meant, basically, two things: having sex and getting high. When Armistead Maupin's *Tales of the City* series began to appear, Peter remembers thinking how low-key it was. The characters' easygoing sexual liaisons and pot smoking were small potatoes to Peter and nowhere near the excitement he regularly sought and found. He would smoke pot, do cocaine, drink five shots of Jack Daniel's, and *then* go out—ready to "bloom." "I felt powerful, as if the whole world were erotic, which San Francisco pretty much was. You couldn't go to a supermarket without feeling the charge of some guy or guys cruising you. I loved it. It was heaven." Heaven consisted of dozens of casual "fuck buddies" and, over the years, hundreds of anonymous sexual contacts. "When I found the baths, it was like they'd been created for me. They were like an overstocked meat market where even the best cuts were free."

Occasionally a "lover" would crop up. This was, to Peter, always a disaster. "A sure way to drain the sex out of a relationship was to get 'involved.' I suspected there was some right man out there for me, but the clinging vines I ended up with weren't him." By the end of the third clinging vine, Jim (a guy Peter dumped because he couldn't stand the "quiet evenings at home" Jim wanted to make out of their relationship), Peter had pretty much given up on "emotional" attachments. He virtually lived in the Folsom Street bars. He drank more than ever, did enormous amounts of cocaine, breathed poppers on dance floors and in back rooms, and developed an attitude that seemed to work for all of it: "Fuck it."

That began to be his attitude toward San Francisco too. "It began to seem too small. I'd had all the guys I wanted to have." He decided to move to New York. He quickly found a roommate through a gay roommate service. Peter was a hot man from San Francisco, which (to New Yorkers) was pretty much the nth degree of erotic. He got a job in a florist shop in the Village ("basically decorating the window—my boss hired me as a lure for customers") and, since it was summer, found himself invited out to the Pines and Cherry Grove in Fire Island by a string of customers, newfound barmates, and the odd man off the street. Peter seemed to be New York's newest stud, and he reveled in it—endless brunches, endless booze, endless dope and cocaine, endless sex. That first summer passed in a euphoric mist, as did the next few years.

By the early eighties (when New York's premiere gay paper, *The Native,* had begun its continuing series about AIDS, which Peter and his friends called "scare tactics"), Peter was no longer the new boy in town, but neither had he turned into an updated Hogarth's *Rake's Progress.* He was still keeping it together. He was now a partner in the florist business and was actually making some good money. He still looked good. And, despite the threat of AIDS that he was hearing about, he kept up a steady stream of sexual partners and kept consuming a steady stream of booze every night. He was determined to keep life the "party" it had always been.

"When I met Tom [Peter's fourth lover], I felt I had New York down pat. I knew how to work it—make money, have good sex, keep high. Tom was an attractive prop—a hot man to be seen with and willing to keep sex open with other guys. When we decided to live with each other, it was like fitting in the last piece of a jigsaw puzzle: now the picture of what I wanted life to look like was complete."

When Tom woke up one morning in a cold sweat, with a deep, hacking cough, Peter remembers being annoyed. ("I didn't want to get the damned *flu.*") When the cough and sweats wouldn't go away, Tom went to the doctor. Peter remembers the afternoon Tom came home with the diagnosis: he had the pneumonia associated with AIDS. "He had this look of total shock. It wasn't like he wanted to cry—he just refused to believe it." Tom had to go into the hospital immediately. His pneumonia escalated wildly and he was put on a respirator. He was dead three days later.

"I couldn't register all this," said Peter. "It was like, one day Tom was here, the next he wasn't. He'd *disappeared.* I couldn't absorb it." A jigsaw piece had fallen out, and to fill that hole in the picture, Peter simply did more of what he'd always done: he *went out.* But now going out had a sharper edge, a frantic quality. Peter couldn't get enough of whatever it was he decided he needed. He couldn't get enough sex at the baths, and bartenders always seemed to take too much time to serve him his next drink. As Peter remembers, "The whole fucking world wasn't moving fast enough."

Soon there wasn't anything he wouldn't do to keep things moving. Once an occasional visitor to the sleaziest backroom clubs in town, he now haunted them. He'd bring a flask of bourbon to suck on while somebody else sucked on him. He got into fist fucking, "water sports," bondage—he became the main event at the Mine Shaft, New York's leading gay after-hours sex palace. Soon there wasn't a time of day when he wasn't taking another slug of bourbon or planning (if not engaging in) his next sexual encounter. One trick with whom he went home drunk turned him on to heroin. Now he'd really found what he was looking for: total release, total oblivion. He picked up a guy who said he got turned on by other people shooting him up, and asked Peter to oblige him. Peter said sure, accompanied him to the guy's rat-hole SRO hotel apartment and discovered he had some of the best dope in New York. Peter gave the guy a triple dose, watched him nod out, pocketed all the drugs in the room, and fled. To this day he doesn't know if the guy ever woke up.

Peter's eventual awakening from the nightmare his life had become was partially because of that incident: somehow, through the dim recesses of the thing his "mind" had become, he realized he might have killed someone. His recovery began at precisely this moment. But, again, it's not his recovery I want to look at. Let's pause again to examine the wealth of data that led to his—and our—dead end.

First, let's do away with any suspicion that Peter's story is a nineteenth-century morality tale, a sort of see-what-hap-pens-when-you're-a-bad-boy? lesson, cranked up a few notches. This is as good a place as any to state a premise: I don't think there's anything wrong with sex and having a good time. I don't especially think there's anything wrong with alcohol, either. And whether I think there's anything wrong with drugs like heroin isn't the point. The point is that whenever we can't *handle* our own behavior—and, conceivably, that could be nonstop churchgoing—we've got a problem. What Peter discovered wasn't that his earlier behavior had been especially "bad": what he realizes now is that it was a cover-up—for something surprising.

"It's the self-hate that floors me now," Peter says. "It floors me because if you had asked me if I 'hated' myself back then, I'd have looked at you cross-eyed. I mean, look at what I was. I was Mr. Gay. I was the hottest thing on the block. They coined the word 'attitude' to describe me. I was completely in control of my life." Peter sighs. "Or so I thought. I should make something clear about Tom's dying of AIDS. I'd never allowed myself to 'love' Tom; I'd never allowed myself to love anybody. So I can't say it hit me in the way you'd think losing a lover would have hit me. What it did was *challenge* me. It was as if, by dying, Tom had dared me to continue living like we both used to do. I guess there was fear buried in me somewhere, but I had spent my life so cut off from my feelings that the only thing that surfaced was something like, 'Oh, yeah? Just try to stop me.' I did everything I could to tempt fate. I was going to squeeze out of life everything I could; I was going to beat all the odds; *I wasn't going to die like Tom.* The rules weren't made for me. If I could get in touch with any feeling at all, it was anger. Like a fighter sticking out his chin as if to say, 'I dare you to hit me.'"

Back to the self-hate: why is that so clear to him today? "Actually, it has to do with the anger I realized I felt. I realized that there were a whole lot of emotions that had never gotten out before. For some reason it crystallized when I read John Rechy's book *Numbers*—the whole 'just one more, one more, one more' sex thing, which I was also doing with booze and dope. It was the realization that I could never, ever, get enough. Something began to break through: what was I trying to escape? I started feeling there was some hysterical, sick, caged animal in me whose lock kept breaking. I never wanted that sick beast to get loose because then people would know what I was hiding—the 'real' me. At the bottom of the sex and booze and drugs was a bottomless pit of fear—fear that I was really nothing, worthless, a piece of shit."

If there's one message I've had drummed into me at all the various Twelve Step meetings I've been to, it's the fact that gay men *grow up* on a diet of self-hate. The degree to which we've internalized the homophobia we've had to deal with from the World Outside is the most saddening discovery I've made. Which is why the triumph of gay men in starting to achieve self-love, of allowing their self-hate to break apart like an iceberg and begin to melt, is such a moving one. To look at Peter, you'd never have thought he had a self-esteem problem: his externals were so bright and smooth. But inside he felt desperately alone. "Hell" is defined differently by each of us—and it manifests itself differently in each of us—but what draws us together is that its *effects* are the same. And just as we need to realize that we've reached hell before we have a hope of getting out of it, we also must take a look at our shame and self-hatred before they have a chance of lifting. It's exactly because we've been so afraid to take that look that we've turned so urgently to the escape hatches of compulsive behavior.

The various bumps in the rug that we've seen have, from one point of view, had several sources: Peter realized that his alcoholism was probably tied to his father being an alcoholic and that he might have had a genetic predisposition to that illness; Grant has come to realize what psychodynamics led up to his overeating and anorexia as well as to his romantic obsessions and emotional rigidities; Matthew sees that his compulsive masturbation was a desperate attempt to assuage his own terribly low self-esteem. All are realizations these men have come to *after* experiencing the breakthrough of surrendering to their addictions. These observations have been made during the relative leisure of recovery; they are not the primary source of recovery. (We'll get a sense of that primary source, as I've been promising, in the next chapter.) But we can reasonably surmise from those observations that we don't choose our particular compulsive activities for no reason. Whether physical or specifically tied to our peculiar psychological backgrounds, there are numerous bases for our choices of addiction.

The revelation, however, is that whatever our detectable, different motives are, we *all* seem to act out from the same basic attitudes. The specific bumps that crop up for us—the various behaviors we choose as ways of acting out our anxiety—do seem to be manifestations of something deeper and more universal than "Daddy drank and so do I." Like Peter, I may have had some sort of genetic predisposition to alcoholism, but it doesn't explain sexual and food addictions quite so clearly. Nor does it explain why I feel such complete identification with a gay man I know whose only Twelve Step program is Debtors Anonymous. Clearly something more is at work than biology—or facile psychology.

What's at work has to do, again, with attitudes common to all of us. They are the real earth from which our bumps grow. Matthew's immense shame, his belief that "good" and "evil" were black-and-white poles and that he was basically "evil"; Grant's swings between grandiosity and self-loathing, his rigid adherences and desperate loves, his hatred of "the rest of humanity"; Peter's frantic, terrified attempts to avoid, at any cost, finding out who he really was: these all come from attitudes—ingrained stances we take toward the world—every one of which seems grounded in deep self-mistrust, if not self-hate.

What makes our attitudes so hard to detect is the mist of our own denial, as well as our fierce attachment to what we are convinced is the only alternative: to act out in the ways we know will bring relief. The net effect—the final package we give ourselves, distilled from all our terrors, all the horror we are sure other people would feel if they only knew who we really were inside, our homophobia, our massive decision that *we can only be the way we are*—is the heartbreaking sense that we're alone. The rules that seem to apply to the rest of the world don't apply to us. We are each of us separate, alone, and inexorably out of reach.

Isolation. It's the terrible fate to which most of us consigned ourselves. What an immense, joyful shock it is to see that isolation vanish—which, in the next chapter, we will begin to do.

Chapter Four
The "Aha!" Moment—The Relief of Surrender

At about 3:15 one October morning, I had the first part of what I call my awakening. At 7:15, when I woke up in my bed and realized, miraculously, that I hadn't been knifed after all by the teenage drug addict I'd propositioned the night before, I had the rest of it.

Here's what happened.

At about 2:45 A.M., I decided to hang around the stoop of my building instead of walking up to face my lover, who I knew would either coldly pretend I wasn't there or mutter, "Where the hell were you tonight?" under his breath. I liked it a good deal more on the cold stone steps outside. I think it was a foggy night—I can't remember, really, because all nights seemed to be foggy—but, anyway, this cute skinny kid came walking down the sidewalk across the street, in front of a vacant lot. I was aware of being very drunk as I pushed myself up off the steps to cross over to him. I had twenty dollars left, a crumpled bill in my pocket, all that was left from the two hundred or so dollars I had started out with that night. I figured if the kid didn't find me exactly devastatingly attractive, I could pay him. Pay him to do what, I wasn't sure. I didn't really care. Who did what to whom didn't matter. The thing was to get us to do something.

He saw me weaving across the street and stood there, waiting, in front of the vacant lot. Good, I thought to myself. Because he was being so cooperative I decided I would go down on him right there under the streetlight, which I was sure he would enjoy. I said, "I want to have sex with you." He said he would do it for money. Obligingly, I reached into my pocket and took out my crumpled bill and gave it to him. Payment now made for services to be rendered, I reached for his crotch. Suddenly, I saw a flash of metal—a knife. "Hey, man," I said, "I paid you." "Don't *fuck* with me, man," he said. I was baffled. This wasn't going according to plan. I was scared. He raised the knife; I saw his arm, needle marks down its taut underside. He caught my eye and hissed out, "Faggot!" Then he turned and ran into the vacant lot behind him. I was left standing there in the light. An interesting thought occurred to me: I hate this. I don't want this to be happening. I was shaken as I realized the kid could have killed me. I stumbled back across the street, a little less drunk. This was the first part of my awakening.

The second part happened when I woke up four hours later in bed. My lover had already gone—something he'd been doing lately so he wouldn't have to speak to me. But for some reason I didn't mind. I was too thunderstruck to mind. If I hadn't been drunk last night, it occurred to me in a brilliant flash, I wouldn't have almost gotten killed. For some reason this gave me tremendous relief. I had figured out what the problem was! It wasn't what I used to tell myself when I'd been sexually rejected before, or when someone told me to shove off after I'd had too much to drink in a bar, or when my boss said she couldn't understand why I couldn't get a three-page report done in three weeks, or when, on the subway, I saw people get up from the seat next to me, moving away because my feet smelled so bad. I had no elaborate excuses—no high psychodrama that was the supposed *real* reason for the interesting messes I kept getting into; no angst based on my tortured past; no existential despair too nuanced to begin to explain. The problem was astoundingly simple: Last night wouldn't have happened if I hadn't been drunk. I suddenly knew I was an alcoholic.

That was the second part of my awakening. And oh, the *relief,* even now, to remember how it felt.

Although I don't know that I could have articulated it at that moment, I've since learned that the simplicity of realizing that I was an alcoholic was an epiphany—and in that epiphany, I believe I experienced nearly everything I needed to know about recovery. In that vast, spacious relief, I experienced surrender; I somehow knew that I could be restored to some kind of sanity, although it wasn't going to be the result of my own piddling will. I felt the full desire to reach out to whomever or whatever could help me back to sanity, and I saw myself, at that moment, for exactly who I was, neither blaming nor judging what I found. I saw all the wreckage and all the hope, a flash of inventory that corroborated my finding—yes, that's what I was, an alcoholic. (I now realize I flashed on the first four Steps of Alcoholics Anonymous.) I experienced, in embryo form, even more. I knew that my recovery depended on honesty—a kind of honesty toward myself and other people I'd never before attempted. And it had to be exactly the kind of honesty I felt toward myself right then, right at that moment. It occurred to me on some level that I'd have to make restitution to the people I'd hurt, and that it wouldn't terrify me.

I know this sounds like an awful lot to have been revealed

in one moment. But, in fact, it came to me on a level beneath words—in a flash of understanding that I was only later able to verbalize. The overwhelming feeling was a sense of having come home—as if I'd finally awakened to who I was and that what I'd found was all right. I don't know anything more relieving than that. *I could be who I was.*

It was, of course, hardly incidental that I also knew I no longer had to drink! I knew, suddenly, that I had a choice— the desire to drink had been lifted from me more completely than I had ever dreamed possible. It wasn't the temporary "Oh, God, I can't bear the thought of alcohol" moment I had had after days of bingeing; the *need* for alcohol had been lifted. I knew there was no reason I'd ever have to pick up a drink again.

Where all of these revelations came from, I've no idea. In fact, I have yet to meet a recovering compulsive person who could tell me where his or her "awakening" really came from. When we found Twelve Step programs, we were told only that what we had experienced was a *gift*—but a gift from whom or what? All that most of us could say is that it seemed to come from a power outside of us, a power greater than ourselves. Some of us called that power "God"—others took the Twelve Step suggestion to call it simply a "higher power," which we could define as we liked.

Does telling all this help anyone else? I don't know. I do know that when I hear other people's experience of awakening to the problem of compulsive behavior, it helps me. Far more than that, it *heals* me. Because the ache I needed so to ease—the ache that got me into bottles and bodies and hells of so many different varieties—that ache is only really assuaged by the magical balm of hearing that other people have felt it too. At least that's part of how the pain lifts. It's such a magical process that I don't know how to analyze it. I only know it happens when I open my heart to other people's pain and allow them to receive mine.

Listening to other people's breakthroughs has taught me that revelations about compulsive behavior seem to have two parts: breaking through denial (*acting out compulsively* is the problem, not whatever you have told yourself "drove you to it"), and realizing you can *survive* without acting out compulsively. This second realization often involves a great, new, welcome sense of hope: you realize not only that you can survive without resorting to compulsive behavior but also that you have a strong inkling you'll *thrive* if you don't fall back on drinking, overeating, sexual promiscuity, or whatever way you feel compelled to act out. You feel freer—lightened by any number of astonishing, unanticipated possibilities.

But revelations don't always, as I've suggested, come in a brilliant instantaneous flash—sometimes they work themselves out over time. And you don't generally stop with the first "revelation," however it came to you. Although that October night and morning constituted my first and (so far) most dramatic breakthrough, I now see that my experience of that moment was really only a beginning, which set in motion a kind of domino effect that I hope will continue for the rest of my life. It let me know what freedom from compulsive behavior feels like—so I'll know it when I need to remember it in the future. And I need to remember it every day.

An essential part of the experience of sobriety seems to be its *ongoing-ness.* You'll shortly re-encounter the men you met in the last chapter, pick up on their stories, and see how varied that ongoing-ness can be. But what seems to be true of all of us is that you don't simply have that first revelation and then stop; in fact, it seems that the *point* of making that first discovery (that you can live—and even want to live—without resorting to compulsive behavior) is to *allow* you to make other discoveries. Sobriety isn't static; it doesn't stop with "Aha! So that's what it's all about. Glad I learned that—now I can go on as before." Sobriety in the recovering people I know is something continuous—and in need of continual renewal.

New revelations have different qualities as you go on.

I smoked three-and-a-half packs of cigarettes a day for fifteen years; nine months into my alcoholic sobriety I was suddenly hit by the new revelation that I didn't want to smoke anymore. It was a marvelous realization that allowed me to see that not only could I survive without doing something self-destructive but also that I *wanted* to survive without it. Although it meant descending into a kind of hell to give it up—I withdrew very badly, reverting to the temper tantrums of a three-year-old, thinking I'd go out of my mind if I didn't have a cigarette, seeing the whole world as a cue to smoke (the worst of this lasted about a week, then it got easier)—it was clear down to the *core* of me what I had to do: stop smoking. My revelation about being an alcoholic was a great teacher: it told me I was *capable* of giving up self-destructive behavior.

But, with sex and food, the problem was (and is) at least superficially thornier. You can't give up food! And I deeply felt that although I had a problem with sexual addiction, there was nothing wrong with sex; I wanted to be able to make it a healthy part of my life, not to excise it forever. My revelations about substances and behaviors that require modification—not eradication—continue even today and, I dearly hope, will go on for the rest of my life. I haven't figured anything out: I simply have learned to ask for guidance, to look to my friends who are struggling with the same addictive issues I am, and to see how and what they're doing.

Some of those friends' stories follow. These are gay men in the trenches—in the front lines—of meeting their addictions. Perhaps that's the first lesson they have taught me: to get out there *into* the front lines, and to start by facing what I'm really doing to myself when I act out compulsively—what it means I think of myself—and to ask myself, again and again, if it's really what I want to be doing. To approach my own compulsive behavior with these questions *invites* revelation. As long as I keep my questioning honest and active and as probing as I know how to make it, I've got a chance to find answers. So far, answers have come—even if they've almost never been what I expected them to be.

SICK PEOPLE GETTING WELL, NOT BAD PEOPLE GETTING GOOD

Peter, as you'll recall, prided himself on being a hot man. He spent most of his adult gay male life living up to what he perceived to be Gay Life's standards of what a hot man was supposed to be and do: have sex and get high, express as little emotion as possible, and stay as far away as possible from anyone or anything that threatened his ego. Peter's cocoon began to unravel when his lover Tom died suddenly of AIDS, but as he's quick to point out, it wasn't because he especially loved Tom. Peter just found more fuel to act out compulsively: he was damned if *he* was going to stop having as much sex and drugs and booze as he could get, just because Tom died. He was damned if *he* was going to die too.

What Peter now realizes is that although Tom's sudden death was in some way connected to why he stepped up his compulsive drinking, dope taking, and sex, that escalation was happening naturally anyway. "Tom's death was like stepping on the gas in a car headed in one direction already," he says. "I'd paved the road I was on long before Tom died. All I started doing then was picking up speed. Not," Peter adds, "that I didn't get some mileage out of Tom's death. When friends of mine started to comment that I was getting out of control, I wasn't above dragging Tom into it—something like, 'Shit, man, if you'd just lost a lover, you wouldn't exactly be in terrific shape either!' I guess I feel some of my strongest sadness around this—that I had to pretend to be upset about Tom in order to justify my drinking, drugging, and sexual excess. The truth is I didn't care about Tom at all. He'd merely turned into one more convenient excuse."

Peter went through his dope stage, and the first real inkling that he was dangerously out of control began to reach him when he realized he might have killed someone. He says, "It wasn't exactly conscious. It was just that I did it without blinking—it was as if it suddenly didn't seem like *me*, whoever the guy was who'd administered that overdose." Peter went on a long drunk after this period, vowing to stay off heroin. And he managed, with the "help" of several gallons of bourbon, to kick his heroin habit. "Dope was the problem, I told myself. That was what was sending me over the edge." Peter more than compensated with booze, to the point of being barred from the Mine Shaft—a pretty difficult thing to do back then, as anyone who went there can tell you. After getting into a fight with the bouncer, where he was punched and kicked out the door, Peter went on a rampage: running through the deserted meat-packing district of the far West Village, tearing at his clothes as he ran, shouting in a drunken rage that everyone in New York was "full of shit," bleeding and stumbling from the beating he'd just gotten, miraculously dodging traffic on the West Side Highway, and ending up at the end of a deserted, rotting pier.

Peter remembers looking into the black water and sobbing. That was where he wanted to be, down in that black water. He didn't throw himself in—he still doesn't understand why—but passed out on the damp, splintered boards of the old pier. He woke up shivering, pelted by rain, on the gray morning after. He had no keys, no wallet, no money, was dressed in only a jockstrap and a torn T-shirt, with no shoes. Blood had dried on his face and plugged his nose; he remembered sneezing in the rain, which made his nose bleed. "I'll never forget what that stream of red looked like running down my chest, mixing with the rain. I'd never reached this point before. This—degradation."

Peter didn't exactly see the light then—all he knew was that he needed help. What he felt was the core sense I'm convinced all compulsive people feel when they are really ready to "recover": total surrender. "I even put it into words, said it aloud. 'I give up. You win.'" Who was "you"? Peter smiles as he recounts this story today. "My Higher Power, of course!" Not that he had any clue of having a "Higher Power" at that moment. All he knew was that he needed something he couldn't give himself: he needed *help* from somebody, something else. He felt he had two choices: dying, or doing something totally different from anything he'd ever done before. "I really didn't want to die," Peter says, "so I decided to look for an alternative."

Peter had been aware of AA. He'd seen gay men walk into a

church on Christopher Street, and he knew it was for such a meeting because he'd heard various drunken men, across the street in a bar he frequented, making snide comments. But he had no idea what to expect. He ended up in a meeting and began his odyssey much the way I did—the way so many other people I know did—in utter *bewilderment*. "Nothing made real sense to me. The Twelve Steps hanging on the wall seemed like some strange fifth-grade homework assignment. Everyone kept clapping at what seemed to me the oddest times. No one 'conversed'—whoever talked got to speak for as long as he wanted, and then someone else talked after him without being interrupted. It was really peculiar." But he stayed. Eventually someone expressed things that Peter had felt. He experienced a rush of identification: "The same immersion in sex and drugs and booze—the same attempts to escape himself—and the guy was good-looking too. Better than good-looking. There was a clear light in his eyes—in so many of the people's eyes in the room—that I noticed right off and that made me a little uncomfortable. It was as if they were those weird kids in *The Village of the Damned,* except they were smiling, understanding, warm eyes." It slowly dawned on Peter that he was where he needed to be. That *this* might be his alternative to death.

Peter's alcoholic sobriety began, and he experienced a lift in his life that was remarkable; he couldn't imagine feeling better than he did. He felt so good, in fact, that he wanted to express how he felt to someone, to make a connection. He was walking through the West Village one weekend afternoon in June, full of this strange, almost enjoyable anxiety, this sense of wanting to "burst"—to get *out* his feeling of elation—when he caught the eye of a blond guy in a muscle T-shirt who was quite obviously willing to "share" whatever

Peter wanted to with him. "It was like something clicked back into an old gear," Peter said. "The hunger I was feeling zeroed in on this guy. I walked over to him, and he invited me up to his place. He offered me cocaine, poppers. I said no, but I really wanted to do them. The guy shrugged, did a couple hits of cocaine, then got down to it with me. He did some poppers while we had sex, and I got a slight whiff of them. It drove me crazy. The old hunger came raging back, and I wanted release." Peter didn't do drugs there and, when he came down from his sex high, realized he really didn't want to do drugs or drink after all. He felt that what he'd been through was probably okay. "I mean, I was 'sober.'" The problem was that the "ache" had come back—the hunger. Sex is where it led him.

As unaccustomed as he was to dealing with the feelings that started to come up now that he wasn't quashing them with booze or drugs, he still felt the reflex to get *rid* of those feelings. Peter soon found himself looking for sex with much of his old urgency. It baffled him, and depressed him.

"Here I was, not drinking or drugging anymore, and yet I was still 'hooked.' In sobriety I couldn't ignore that I was putting myself in danger of AIDS; in fact, it would be a wonder if I didn't have AIDS incubating in me already, and so I was probably putting other people in danger too. The stuff I was learning in AA made this realization really painful. Here they were talking about being honest, open, and willing—about looking at the consequences of my actions—and here I was in the grip of something that was making me go back on all that. It's true that being sober in an alcohol and drug sense usually made me have safer sex. But, to be honest, there were times when I gave in and—what's the polite term?—exchanged bodily fluids." Peter realized, gradually, that he was again out of control. "What the hell had happened? I thought I was 'working my program' in AA, but this other thing had cropped up just as urgently as alcohol ever had. I found myself going out cruising every chance I got. It was embarrassing when I'd see someone from AA on the street and he'd check me out in what I thought of as my sex clothes. I'd feel exposed, as if I were caught committing some crime."

This was about the time Peter started sneaking into gay porno movie houses. "The darkness—the anonymity—it felt perfect to hide there. I tried to rationalize that I was just trying to 'discharge' energy. But my sexual obsessiveness was something a lot fiercer than that." Peter found himself on his knees in a toilet in a Hell's Kitchen movie house with somebody shoving some poppers under his nose, the liquid burning his skin. With some stranger's cock in his mouth, he began to feel violently ill—sick to his stomach. "It wasn't the fact that I was about to suck some guy's cock. It was that I was once again completely out of control." He started to cry, right then and there. Something broke in him. For the second time in his life, he had hit bottom.

Peter had to face a brutal realization: sex was as potent a drug to him as bourbon or heroin had been. But what was he supposed to *do* about sex? At first he thought, Hell, I'll just be celibate. I can't handle it anymore. If abstinence worked for alcohol and drugs, wouldn't it work here too? After about two weeks of enforced celibacy—no masturbation, no anything—Peter felt as if he were going to explode. "It wasn't even that I was horny," he says now. "I just couldn't contain my feelings. I couldn't stand being in my skin. I felt this tremendous need to get *out* of myself." Peter doubled up on AA meetings and got a little relief. "It helped to realize that Bill W. seemed to be addicted to womanizing; there was so much in the Big Book about dealing with destructive sexual urges." But Peter still felt as if something was eating him alive. He looked around an AA room one day and focused on a man he'd always liked listening to—a guy whose sobriety he respected. He tentatively approached him and asked him if he might act as his sponsor—the person Twelve Step programs encourage you to hook up with to answer your questions, to help you along in sobriety, and to share with on a more intimate level. The guy said yes, and over coffee in a diner on the West Side of Manhattan ("not far from where I'd last acted out sexually," Peter says), he poured his heart out to his new sponsor. Amazingly, the guy didn't blink. He even said he understood. More than that, he'd been through a lot of the same things and was still grappling with sex too. He told Peter there were other programs designed to help with sexual addiction. Peter wanted to jump up from the table and find one that instant. It turned out there was a Sexual Compulsives Anonymous (SCA) meeting that night, and Peter's sponsor took him there.

Sex is one of the most exasperating great mysteries of life. Nowhere are we more primally connected to fear of intimacy, to our own self-hatred and homophobia, than in sex; nowhere are we more aware of that craving I call an "ache." (If there is an ache to be eased, it's here.) Peter, like just about every other compulsive human being I've ever met, was impatient. At first he couldn't accept that there were no clean, across-the-board guidelines he could follow, such as "Do this and you'll be sexually sober," the way there seemed to be in AA and NA. He was not especially encouraged to "give up" sex—unless, after careful reflection and discussion with other people who shared his sexual addiction, he thought that a period of abstinence might help him. He was encour-

71

to develop a "sex plan"—a series of guidelines that
ned "sexual sobriety" personally for him. With the help
of other "sex addicts," he was encouraged to look, with all
the honesty and openness and willingness he tried to bring to
his AA recovery, at what the *likely* consequences of having sex
would be in a variety of circumstances, and then to choose
his own path—with the goal of feeling peace in himself.

This seemed an impossible task at first. Peter quickly realized he had no clue as to what he really wanted, no ideas as to
what might ease the ache in his *soul* for serenity, completion,
contact. Especially contact. He says now that the only part of
his ache he could define was the urge to connect to somebody—the immense need for affection, for release in someone else's arms—for "love." This was a revelation to Peter,
and a profoundly uncomfortable one. "Sex was completely
separate from love in my life. It never really occurred to me
to link the two at all; in fact, that's why I was always disap-
pointed with having a lover. The moment caring entered the
picture, desire left. Why was I so divided? I still didn't know. I
only know that now that I've given myself a little time to be
with myself, I've discovered that my feelings won't make me
explode the way I thought they would. I've given myself the
time to realize that what I'm really after isn't sex at all. I'm
after release. A feeling of oneness. I'm after what I can only
say, because I can't think of a better word, is 'love.'" Peter
laughs. "Or as a recovering addict friend of mine—who happens to be a clergyman—says, 'My people call it God.'"

You don't have to drag in God to define more clearly what
our cravings are all about; the important point is that when
you allow yourself, as Peter is learning to allow himself, to
tolerate a craving rather than immediately act out on it, you
can learn some interesting things about what it's really urg-

ing you to do. Peter's task isn't, as he once thought it was, to flee from his craving—to try to stamp it out, ignore it, white-knuckle his way through it until it passes. It's to find ways to satisfy it! We grow up hating our cravings—which recovering gay compulsive men are starting to realize is exactly the opposite of what will help us. It seems that if, instead, we learn to *love* our cravings—trust that being "hungry" is not a sin but rather an indication that we do need something—we've got a chance of finding out what will truly satisfy us.

The lesson that Peter and other recovering compulsive people have taught me is that the very ache I try to escape from through compulsive behavior is the ache I need to feel. That ache, if I pay enough attention to it, if I follow its dictates without fear and with an open heart and mind, can be my truest guide. It can lead me to a deeper and more lasting satisfaction than I've ever been able to find in booze, drugs, sex, or food. The tragedy of compulsive behavior isn't that it's an unspeakable sin or moral failing: it's that it prevents us from going the full distance necessary to reach the answer we are really after. This is a crucial point because it takes away all guilt, all moral condemnation, all the shame we feel about acting out. When we can learn to see ourselves compassionately enough to realize that what we are expressing in compulsive behavior is an urgent craving to find *peace,* then we can begin to focus on truly finding that peace. When we're honest with ourselves, we see we can't find peace in the places where we've been looking. So the obvious answer is to look elsewhere.

Why are we so afraid to take that look?

Peter and I keep bumping into that fear, and so does every other gay compulsive man I know. Even when we have proven to ourselves that "acting out" is bad for us—even when we have discovered what a relief it can be to live life without resorting to our compulsive escape hatches—it's still hard, sometimes, to keep renewing our commitment to stay sober. Part of the problem, says Peter, is "adjusting to the fact that your hungers keep coming back." Peter gave Sexual Compulsives Anonymous what he calls "a good, healthy try" for a few weeks. "I really did start to feel better—not so frantic. I found I could actually calm myself down when I felt the urge to go out and look for sex, and I could try to sense how much was just the need to relieve anxiety or the need to *be* with someone. What a revelation to know that you can relieve anxiety and be with people without tearing off each other's clothes! It was great to be able to call 'time out' for myself and take a clearer look at what was going on beneath the urge to act out."

Then, however, Peter accidentally uncovered his old membership card to one of the two remaining bathhouses in New York City. "I stared at that thing. Months before I'd stuffed it into the back of a drawer in my desk. Ironically, I was cleaning up my desk to vent some anxiety. I'd wanted to act out sexually that day, so I figured I'd try what my sponsor suggested: attempt to turn that energy into something positive. At least, I thought, I'd have a clean desk." But coming upon the card totally threw Peter. "Just to see it was like having a shot of bourbon." Peter started to fantasize about the times he went to the baths: "How exciting it was, how many hot men there were, even at that moment, waiting—just hanging around, waiting for me." Peter put the card in his pocket. He looked out the window at the gray Saturday morning, then down at his messy desk. "Damn, I thought. What the hell is wrong with enjoying myself? I mean, it's not like I'm a little kid who has to ask permission to do what he wants to do. What's wrong with having a little sex if I want to? Who am I hurting, as long as I keep it safe?" Suddenly the whole notion of Sexual Compulsives Anonymous struck him as ridiculous: "A bunch of tight-ass schoolmarms whose only real problem is that they felt guilty for being gay. Well, I thought, I'm damned if I'm going to feel guilty for being gay. I can have sex whenever I want! It's my goddamn right."

Having worked himself up to this zealous pitch, he rode on that energy all the way up to the baths. He shoved his money at the cashier, impatient to be let in, given a towel, shown to his room. Everyone seemed to be taking so much *time.* ("Damn," Peter remembers thinking, "get me *in* there.") A laid-back attendant escorted him to his room; Peter hurried him, shoving a tip into his hand, pushing him away as he did so. He ripped at his clothes to get them off, popping a button on his shirt, then bunched them under the cot. He propped up his pillow, opened the door, sat back. And he waited. It was only 10:30 in the morning—virtually no one was there. A defeated-looking old man slowly walked by the open door and tentatively looked in. Peter gave him an impatient negative nod; the man accepted it. Obviously it wasn't the first no he'd received in his life. He plodded on. No one else walked by for an endless minute or two. Peter sprang up from his cot, took his keys, grabbed for his towel, hastily tied it around his waist, and then stomped out into the corridor. All the doors in the hall were shut. He walked down another corridor. One door was open. He looked into the dimly lit room and saw a young kid sprawled out asleep, half on, half off his bed. Peter knew that passed-out look very well: quaaludes, probably. He went to the little room where they usually showed videotapes of porno flicks. It seemed to be between films—there were nothing but gray dots of static on the screen. A plump middle-aged man sat on the bench in front of the screen anyway. He was obviously waiting too. He looked up hopefully at Peter and patted the front of his towel. Peter abruptly turned and walked away, returning to his room. He opened the door, then closed it behind him. He felt like crying. This, he remembers thinking to himself, is *not* what I want.

However, that wasn't the last time Peter tried the baths, even after another few weeks of SCA meetings. As long as he held on to his baths card, he was in trouble. It was, for him, like keeping a bottle of bourbon under the kitchen sink— out of sight, sometimes, but never completely out of mind. And sometimes he got what he thought he was after at the baths—the old release. "But it wasn't the same. I couldn't give myself over to it. I was too damned sober to give in to it completely, or for long." Peter finally experienced yet another level of surrender. "I started to realize, once again, that it was the acting out that was making me miserable. Not sex itself. I didn't want to get out of control again. I didn't want to feel that terrible despair. And I *was* starting to feel it."

Peter finally took a scissors, as well as a deep breath of resolution, cut up his card, and threw it away. He has started to "count days"—which Twelve Step programs encourage you to do to celebrate each day that you maintain sobriety, and as a reminder that you can accomplish this only one day at a time. He has started listening harder at SCA meetings and participating more himself. He has also stepped up his AA involvement and has begun to see how wonderfully recovery in one program can feed recovery in another. He has begun to get a glimmer of the kind of freedom he is really after, and he has seen it in the other gay men who "slipped" too but kept coming back anyway. "Nobody ever got better by acting out" is Peter's terse summation of what he's learned so far. "I haven't heard one person who's come back say, 'Hey, you should try it again!'" Peter is trying to tolerate his cravings—to see what lies *beyond* acting out. At the best moments, he says, "I experience a deeper peace and self-acceptance than I've ever known. I'm starting to date men now—something I'd never done before. I'm starting to let up on myself too. I'm allowing myself to feel what I'm feeling—and not running away every time it gets tense." At the worst moments, "it's still a bummer. I don't know that I can keep from acting out for the rest of my life. The only thing I've learned is that I can usually keep myself from acting out right *now*. If you string enough nows in a row, you've got a day. And then, maybe, two days. And so it goes. Nobody said it would be easy getting used to being me—much less learning to love myself. But I guess I acknowledge that's what I want to do— love myself. Slowly I find I cringe a little less at the thought. And slowly I'm coming to realize that the only thing acting out does is get in my way. It stops me from going forward. Keeps me from what I'm finding I really do want. Serenity."

Making the connection that there *are* bumps in your rug— that, as we learned in the last chapter, we can choose an almost infinite number of ways to escape—allows you to take a look, again, at the nature of the cravings that underlie all those escape tactics. What we seem to find is that being "with" our cravings can ultimately lead us to recovery—not doing everything we can to block them out, truncate them, get rid of them prematurely. When we start to see that our craving is really for something deeper and better and more satisfying than what we can find in quick anonymous sex or a bottle of bourbon (or any of the other escape tactics Peter and the rest of us may be drawn to choose in the future—more *will* crop up, you can be fairly warned), we also learn to ease up on the sin factor. Many people have what I have learned is a profound misconception about Twelve Step recovery. Because of some of the higher power language, talk about spiritual awakenings, learning to make amends, and any number of other religious-sounding suggestions you will hear in meetings, you may get the quick idea that you've got to suffer religious conversion before you can take part in the proceedings. In fact, the only requirement for membership in AA or any other Twelve Step program is the desire to stop whatever activity the program has been formed to help you recover from—whether it is drinking, having compulsive sex, eating compulsively, working compulsively, spending compulsively, and the rest. Twelve Step programs are expressly based on *desire*—not deprivation.

"We are sick people getting well, not bad people getting good," I'm reminded again and again at the meetings I go to. We're in pursuit of fulfillment—not retribution for our "sins." I'm learning to be grateful for my hungers; they are what lead me (when I let them) to a stronger sense of who I am and how I might fulfill the deeper desire for completion and peace of mind from which my compulsions cut me off. But, *whoa boy,* it's hard. In attempting to face and tolerate my compulsive urges, I'm going against some deeply ingrained assumptions, assumptions I've clung to most of my life. Sex is dirty and furtive. You can't get enough food—ever. Only alcohol can help you relax. The only way to lose weight is to take uppers. Stay up all night and every night until that project is done. Push yourself. Pull yourself. Make yourself behave. Whether pro or con, whether in pursuit of pleasure or slapping my own wrist for indulging in too much pleasure, when I'm left to my own devices I'm in a terrible tug-of-war in which the only two sides are Act Out and Hate Yourself for Acting Out. It is exhausting.

That I don't have to depend on *one* revelation to show me the way out is one of the most welcome lessons I've learned. There are more revelations as you find deeper levels of "surrender." Peter has shown us a few of his own. I've given you my October morning of the soul. Now let's briefly take a look at Grant and Matthew.

SOME LESSONS OF HUNGER

We left Grant in the hospital, waking up angry, still furious at the world's inadequacies and other people's inability to appreciate what an extraordinary creature he was. He then plummeted into a terrible despair. Everything seemed to collapse at once—all hope vanished. He felt worthless. His depression was severe enough that the hospital would release him only on the condition that he receive outpatient psychological care. "A measure," Grant says he thought, "that had more to do with legal hospital policy than any genuine desire to help me." His enforced therapy did not look promising. "It was a clinic full of homeless, jobless people, real fringe types. Overworked, jaded social workers seemed to process everyone through like so many heads of cattle. With the view of humanity I'd nurtured most of my life, this seemed somehow poetically apt. I almost enjoyed the Kafkaesque masochism of it all. It simply corroborated what I felt about most of the world: it was full of hopeless, stupid, inept, semi-evolved animals stumbling over one another."

The obvious distance Grant perceived between himself and these "lowlifes" enabled him to regain his belief in his own superiority. He was suitably haughty when he met the prematurely gray-haired woman to whom he was assigned for therapy. He asked her how many sessions hospital red tape required him to suffer through. His social worker looked up wearily and said that if he never came back again they'd probably never catch up with him, given the bureaucratic difficulties of catching up on anything, but if he wanted to be *helped,* she'd do what she could. That's why she was there, she reminded him. Grant smiled condescendingly and said it also didn't hurt to be gainfully employed, did it?

"The lady had obviously had it up to here—not just with me, I'd just walked in, after all—but with the dozens of ingrates she'd dealt with that day, all the days before that day, all the weeks and months she'd been stuck in her office. She blew up at me. 'Look,' she said, 'you came into this hospital half dead. Either you want to die or you want to live. If you want to die, leave. If you want to live, shut your trap for a moment and listen to what I've got to say!'" Grant was so taken aback he didn't go into one of his usual "how dare you speak to me this way?" huffs. He says he almost felt like he was in a movie—with Joan Blondell letting-'er-rip. He looked at his raging social worker with wide eyes, and a tiny bit of respect.

"She must have sensed my attitude change because she softened a little," Grant says. "She said it was pretty clear I had an eating disorder and asked me what I thought about that. I thanked her for her diagnosis and told her I'd simply been depressed over a broken love affair. She said most people with eating disorders denied they had them. I again calmly explained to her that the real problem had to do with an

unhappy romantic situation and would she kindly stop talking about food. She said, no, she wouldn't stop talking about
food since that was so obviously what we had to deal with
first. I told her I appreciated her concern, but I obviously
needed someone with more experience than she evidently
had, perhaps a psychiatrist, someone trained in more ortho-
dox analytical techniques than she seemed to be. She said if I
ever decided to cut the crap and face up to what was really
going on in my life, I might want to contact the organization
she was scribbling down on a small piece of paper. She handed
me the paper, and I looked down to Overeaters Anonymous
and a number. I told her she was probably the least compe-
tent therapist I'd ever met, and, if I got around to it, I might
initiate legal proceedings against her. I certainly would if she
opened her mouth about 'eating disorders' ever again in my
presence. She shrugged and wished me good luck. I got up
and showily ripped the piece of paper she'd handed me into
shreds. I then walked out the door.

"Overeaters Anonymous! I thought to myself. My god, had
she *looked* at me? She thinks I look fat? And then I remembered
that I was 131 pounds—6 pounds over my limit. Maybe I did
look fat. I *had* gained weight from all that awful hospital food.
What an insulting bitch she was! Talk about what happens
when you let *anyone* get to be a therapist. No wonder the mental health system was disintegrating, with asses like that
employed in it." Grant can't quite explain why he found himself asking directory assistance for the number of Overeaters
Anonymous that afternoon. He knows he was out to prove
that therapist wrong. Perhaps he'd go to a meeting, take
notes, and write a scathing excoriation of all the anonymous
Twelve Step cults that were insidiously taking over the country—and name his therapist as one of their obvious plants! He

steeled himself for a Moonie brainwashing session; he enjoyed the prospect of savaging the whole show. He worked himself up to an almost enjoyable nervous pitch, anticipating how he'd blow the lid off Overeaters Anonymous. Without betraying this venomous zeal, he managed to extract the place and time of a meeting that night from an innocuous-sounding male voice that answered the number directory assistance had given him. It was in the basement of a church to which he used to go for Bach chorale concerts. He was appalled. Imagine a conspiracy like that going on in the basement! he thought to himself. Bach would roll over in his grave. There was no bottom to Grant's indignation.

He dressed carefully that night, in slimming black. He didn't want to look as if he needed to lose weight, even if his weight was over the 125-pound limit he'd set for himself. He wanted to flaunt his difference from the roomful of fatties he was sure he'd find. He was a man with a mission: he would single-handedly wake them up to the brainwashing they were receiving. He paused in front of his full-length mirror. Was that a slight bulge around his middle, swelling his black T-shirt? Maybe he'd better change into the loose black sweater. As always, Grant didn't dare look into the mirror when he pulled his shirt off; he was afraid he might catch a glimpse of a ripple of fat, and that would have devastated him. So he closed his eyes as he changed from shirt to sweater and only then surveyed the difference. Yes, he thought, better. They won't see I really do need to lose weight.

Grant got to the meeting late. He was unaccountably shy. He almost didn't walk in, decided he *was* on a mission, and since he'd never backed off from a resolution before, resolved to go through with this one. The meeting was already in progress. Grant looked in some wonder around the room.

There were people of every size, from svelte to overweight, much, Grant thought, like *real* people! He sat at the back of the room. When he focused on the speaker, an attractive, perfectly normal-size man in his late twenties, Grant wondered if he'd happened onto the wrong meeting. These people—and especially this man—weren't particularly fat. He began to pick up the speaker's message midstream. The guy was talking about how he used to hate himself for ever feeling hungry. The rest of the audience laughed warmly, identifying. "After I'd lost fifty pounds the second time," the speaker continued (Grant was astonished: this slim man had lost fifty pounds more than once?), "every time I had a cup of *tea* I'd worry about whether the water would make me bloat up. Then I'd figure, what the hell, I had no control over looking bloated, my body was obviously dead set against me, there was nothing I could do about anything, and I might as well give myself *some* kind of pleasure since I obviously wasn't going to experience the pleasure normal people felt, being loved because they were slim and beautiful and all the things I knew I'd never be." The speaker ran out of breath after this run-on sentence and everyone laughed—with him, not at him. "Whew!" he continued. "All that so I could get back to eating Ring Dings!" The room was again filled with that same, wonderful laughter—the way any group of people laughs when someone pricks a fat pretension and reveals a naked truth. "I wanted to devote my life to Ring Dings, and so I did. And the fifty—make that sixty—pounds came back on for the *third* time.

Grant was stupefied. Word by word, the guy was stripping off every pretense. He was actually telling a roomful of people how he felt! Baring himself like that in public! And no one made fun of him. No one walked out. They seemed to love it. That was the feeling—the odd and uncomfortable feeling—that Grant couldn't escape in this cramped church basement: everybody loved that guy for telling the truth about himself. It was unnerving.

The notion that you could tell the truth to anybody was profoundly unsettling to Grant—but letting a whole roomful of people in on what you felt, what you were really going through, was beyond his comprehension. During the rest of the meeting, Grant was stunned by the honesty he heard from the men and women in the room. He was especially struck by the guilt everyone was struggling with about all of their "hungers," not just for food. "I grew up thinking I didn't deserve anything" was one typical plaint. "And so I got the idea I had to steal—and hoard—and get more of everything I could—just so I'd never run out, never be hungry, never be empty again. That was why I couldn't stop eating." Grant thought back to his high-fat days when a pound of bacon would disappear at breakfast, two pints of Häagen-Dazs would disappear midmorning, and three cheeseburgers with fries would disappear at lunch. He'd been out of control. And, what about now? Was he any more in control now? He heard one woman talk about the self-hatred she felt beneath her furious dieting regime. She cried when she said she almost picked up some diet pills that afternoon—she was sure her boyfriend would leave her if she gained so much as an ounce. People walked up to her after the meeting, held her, comforted her, talked to her. Grant was stung again. He thought of his own furious regimens. Everything he was hearing at this meeting was striking reverberant chords. It was both wonderful and terrible. He was physically shaking by the end of the meeting. Then the man who had "qualified"—which Grant learned was the word Twelve Step programs used for "spoke" (it meant telling your story as to why you "qualified" for the program)—walked up to him and put a hand on his shoulder. "Are you new?" he asked. Grant blinked and fought back a terrible dry feeling in this throat. "You don't know *how* new," he managed to croak. The guy asked him to join a group going out for coffee. Grant amazed himself by saying yes.

You can tolerate your hunger: that was the big revelation for Grant that night. The fact that you could do something about hunger—besides hate it and flee from it, or gorge yourself mindlessly until you got so sick or numb that you didn't feel it anymore—was astounding news. It ultimately led Grant on a tour of more than Overeaters Anonymous: he found a Twelve Step group for anorexics that showed him the flip side of the coin. When he was ready to investigate the "people" side of his compulsive urges more fully, he found himself going to Romantic Obsessives and CODA (Co-dependents Anonymous) meetings. Today, "surrendering on deeper and deeper levels to hungers I can't control, feelings I can't keep from coming up, I'm discovering that there *isn't* some bottomless pit I'll fall into if I don't eat or obsess about someone—that there's something buoyant waiting to break my fall and bring me up again. That 'something' is partially the people I'm allowing to get to know me in meetings, but it's also a 'something' I can't describe so easily. I used to groan at the word 'spiritual,' but that comes closest to describing what the help I'm receiving feels like. Spirituality doesn't seem quite so intimidating anymore. It's simply a word for a realm I'm becoming more and more conscious of as I get more and more help. I'm finding so much beyond the urges and problems and physical reality I used to think were the whole show. I'm learning there's so much more."

Grant still sometimes gets spooked when he catches himself talking like this; the old, rigid self is so ingrained that its ghost continues to haunt and sometimes direct him. Getting sober is a softening process, and when we are so used to being rigid, we can sometimes choke with fear at the thought of letting go—surrendering. Grant still collides with that fear as he faces each new moment of "softening." But he has an "Aha!" moment—a new insight—every time he allows himself to soften, to let go, to become receptive. That's what he brings to our definition of revelation about compulsive behavior: "When you let go, you won't fall—you won't die. You'll be buoyed up. You'll be taken care of."

The *trust* it takes to live according to that belief is—no doubt about it—enormous. Learning to love something you used to hate (yourself, for example) requires a 180-degree turn most of us can't conceive of maneuvering. The joy is in discovering we don't have to make that maneuver on our own; in fact, we couldn't if we tried. What Peter and Grant have just shown us are examples of the strangest paradox of recovery: it is only by admitting defeat that we triumph. Let's now see Matthew's version of getting to that revelation. What he has to tell us about *guidance* should enrich the sense we are already getting that you don't have to accomplish all this on your own.

WHAT THE MIND CAN'T DO, SOMETHING ELSE CAN

We left Matthew, last chapter, just as he was beginning to discover that his tactic of compulsive masturbation was failing him. ("It wasn't working anymore.") Matthew voluntarily turned to a therapist for help—his despair was so great that he felt it was either that or commit suicide. "What my therapist wanted me to do was rechannel my energy into something 'healthier.'" This sounded wise enough, so Matthew made himself stay longer at work, take on long-term, high-pressure projects that would exhaust him so that the idea of masturbating somewhere would be less appealing. For a while it worked—almost too well. Matthew's compulsivity shifted to his job. He was obsessive about details, unpredictably blowing up at people he didn't think were moving fast or efficiently enough—a personality change that his boss noticed with some approval but his co-workers liked a good deal less. Matthew was turning into a real pill. He made one of these co-workers stay until 9:00, 10:00, 10:30 one night, laboring to reach a deadline that Matthew himself had imposed, and the co-worker finally snapped. "*You* can drive yourself crazy if you want, but I'm not playing along. Go ahead and get me fired. I'm going home to bed." This was someone Matthew had always liked and gotten along with—he'd always seen him as an ally. He was devastated by the co-worker's anger and abrupt departure. He found himself in his office, alone, one light over his desk, with piles of half-finished work meticulously laid out for completion. Something in Matthew screeched to a dead halt.

"I couldn't stand it anymore. Nothing was working. I looked at all the careful collating and editing and organizing I was doing, and suddenly it all seemed stupid. What the hell was I doing all this for?" Matthew barely managed to resist the urge to shove all that paper on the floor. He sank into a swivel chair at his desk. The idea of masturbating hit him dimly. He thought, What the hell, what does it matter what I do? He halfheartedly unzipped and pulled out his cock. He remained limp. No fantasy tugged at him. Nothing was left. He felt absolutely barren. He had a vivid picture of himself, "alone in that dark office, sitting at my desk with my damned cock in my hand. It seemed, somehow, a symbol of my whole life. I was a master of the inappropriate gesture. I fit in nowhere." Suicide seemed a logical alternative, but Matthew was suddenly too tired to imagine how he would accomplish it. He'd go home and think of how to kill himself the next day. That, at least, gave him a little hope. He at least had the solace of knowing he could get out of his stupid, barren, lonely life and quit keeping up the charade that anything meant anything.

Matthew collapsed into bed and woke up no less depressed the next morning. The idea of ending it all was as appealing in the bright light of day as it had been late at night. True to his habits, however, he knew he'd have to keep his appointments that day. He'd kill himself after he'd done all the things he'd promised he'd do.

One of the appointments Matthew decided to keep was with his therapist. He didn't plan to tell him about his suicidal thoughts; he didn't want the interference he was sure he would get. But, as he says now, "I must have had some dim, half-conscious hope that maybe my therapist would pull a rabbit out of a hat—come up with a cure-all answer to how lousy I felt about myself." As it happens, Matthew's therapist, who was a mild, unexcitable little man, was his usual quiet, listening self—no new sparks promised to fly on this particular day. Matthew made some noncommittal remarks about how work wasn't going too well. His therapist asked him if he wanted to talk about it. Matthew said there was nothing to talk about. The session proceeded at this snail's pace, the two men exchanging quiet monosyllables, Matthew's depression slowly filling the room like a fog. Time was nearly up.

But, suddenly, Matthew didn't want to leave. He wanted to tell this man that he was planning to kill himself. Then he felt the beginning of a question: "Did wanting to share the fact that I planned to kill myself mean I really didn't want to go through with it?" With seven minutes remaining in the session (Matthew knew because he kept glancing at his digital watch to see how much time he had left—at first he wanted the time to fly; now he prayed for it to stop), he turned to face his therapist and tried to formulate words. No sound came out of his throat. He felt something strange rise in his chest—the beginnings of a sob. Matthew couldn't remember the last time he'd cried. Sounds started to wrack out of him, like some machine, rusty from neglect, choking into gear. He was finally able to say something: *"I don't want to die."*

It took all of Matthew's thirty-five years to say something this definite—something this true and simple about himself. The struggle in him wasn't what he might have said it was that morning, or the day before, or three years before. The struggle wasn't really between masturbation and work; it wasn't the result of having no friends or even of his self-hatred, which he knew was at the very bottom of what he felt about himself. It was the struggle to give himself permission to live—to want to live. He finally gave himself over to a great, simple decision: *he wanted to live, not die.*

This is the great simple, decision made by every compulsive person who seeks recovery—or, for that matter, by any sick person who wants to get well. It's a bedrock decision to live. It is an enormous geological shift in perspective, one that does nothing less than reverse a negative pole to a positive one. Matthew says he began to feel a flood of healing, of relief, when he surrendered to life. "Suddenly it didn't matter that my life was a wreck, that everything was in pieces. The only thing mattered was I wanted to go on. I wanted to *exist*. I know it sounds strange—or at least I expected it would sound strange back then—but I'd gone through the motions of my life not really accepting that I was alive, that I was really there. It would always amaze me, for example, when days or weeks or months later anyone would remember something I'd said or done. I couldn't accept that I'd actually had an impact on anything. Because I'd felt such great shame about myself, I saw myself as a shadow—something that slunk in and out of view, something that took up as little space as it could, something that didn't matter, that nobody took notice of. I guess my compulsive masturbation was the only act I felt was *real*—it was the only time I felt I existed. I began, for the first time, to have some compassion for myself and not to hate myself so much for acting out, but rather to accept that I was just trying to make a connection—feel something—feel like I mattered, that I really was on this plant."

Such a rush of words was unusual for Matthew, or at least it had been in the old days. Now, however, this inner decision—this movement toward life—seems to have opened a floodgate. "I've learned so much. It was a while before I found out I could get help from Twelve Step programs, but because I kept talking to my therapist about the feeling of 'surrender' I had had, he came up with an idea. He had never heard of Sex and Love Addicts Anonymous [SLAA] or any of the other Twelve Step groups having to do with compulsive sex, but he thought I might get something out of going to open meetings of Al-Anon. I was so receptive at that point to doing anything that I was happy to go." Al-Anon was a wonderful awakening. "My parents weren't alcoholic, but they had unpredictably given and withdrawn love in the same ways I heard people in Al-Anon describe the alcoholics in their lives. I had felt at the mercy of my parents' whims throughout my childhood, and I identified completely with the tales of physical and emotional abuse I heard about in meetings. I was riveted by the recovery I saw going on—by the radically new notion of 'keeping the focus on yourself.' I saw people struggling to take responsibility for their own actions, for the likely *consequences* of their own actions."

There was more Matthew found: "I saw people turning to one another for help. This was maybe the most astonishing thing of all, that you didn't have to do it all on your own. That you didn't have to depend on your own will, on your own wits, for survival and direction. I'd grown up with an idea that had been battered into me forever: it's up to *you* to figure out what to do with your life. But I saw these people turn to other sources for direction—to one another and to something else, something they called their 'higher power.' Something was responsible for recovery that had nothing to do with will, with the power of any one person's mind or intellect." Matthew quoted somebody who had really put this in a nutshell for him: "The guy said that his mind was a fine instrument as long as it was given a purpose—directions to carry out. But the mind isn't equipped to come up with that purpose itself. When you ask your intellect, "What should I do?" The eventual answer is always, 'I don't know.' The mind can't know its own direction, just like a car can't know where to go without a driver. You seem to *get* that driver, that direction, from something different, from figuring it out. You get it from your heart. You get it from God."

These are insights I've condensed from what took Matthew a long time to amass, but right from the start, he knew he was in the right place—or at least asking the right questions. "I got some wonderful things from Al-Anon—the new sense of direction I've already talked about, the feeling that I didn't have to do everything on my own. But I didn't speak at a meeting for a very long time. I really didn't think I belonged since I wasn't there for what seemed to be the usual reason—I didn't have an alcoholic in my life." After several weeks of meetings, a kindly man walked up to him, introduced himself, and asked Matthew how he liked the meeting. Matthew beamed but admitted that he wasn't sure he belonged. The man told him something that has stuck with Matthew ever since: "I thought I was coming here for the alcoholic in my life the first time I came," he said, "but now I know I'm coming for myself. If it's helping you, you're in the right place." This gave Matthew courage to tell a little more about himself, first to this man, then in the meeting itself. He still didn't talk about his compulsive masturbation, but he was able to see the unhealthy dependencies he'd developed in work and with his parents—numerous unsuspected ways he was attaching himself negatively to people.

Matthew finally discovered the existence of SLAA—Sex and Love Addicts Anonymous—from the chairperson of his Al-Anon meeting, who gave him a list of Twelve Step groups that met locally. Matthew was riveted by the listing: "Could this really exist—a perfect program for me?" Then his heart sank. "I never could talk about my problem to straight people; at least at that moment, it seemed impossible. But maybe I would go and just listen." He went to his first SLAA meeting full of trepidation, and when the guy who was to qualify was introduced, Matthew braced himself for some long tale of womanizing to which he suspected he'd never be able to relate. The guy started talking about how he'd always hated

himself for being gay. That the only solace he could find anywhere was in masturbation. Matthew couldn't believe what
he was hearing. He felt simultaneous urges to laugh and cry.
He had come home.

Not every person who spoke at slaa had a story so near to
Matthew's, but he saw quickly that it didn't matter. The *feelings* they were talking about were so familiar that it seemed
they'd been tugged out of his soul.

I've offered this chapter as an "explanation" of the "Aha!"
moment—a suggestion of what the relief of surrender can
feel like. I don't know that such an explanation is possible—
at least not if you're looking for circumstances that exactly
mirror your own. What Matthew discovered first in Al-Anon
and then in slaa was a current that connected him to other
people far more deeply than he ever thought possible. The
details of his experience, the bumps in his rug, the specific
ways he learned to view himself and the world, are, as he
now says, "My particular coloration—like the color of my
hair or eyes or skin." But they constituted a thin membrane
over a heart and a soul and a *craving* that reflects those of
every human being with whom he comes in contact (not
only every other compulsive human being). The "Aha!"
moment for Matthew is the rushing sense that he is connected to others, that he is a human being—not a slug, not
a rat, not a shadow. It is also the full, unanticipated acknowledgment that he wants to explore his connections to others—that he wants to live.

As we've seen with Peter and Grant and myself, that decision to live is only the beginning—a glorious, necessary,
healing beginning, and a doorway into a new realm. Perhaps
you've already begun to taste the marvelous *sufficiency* that

recovery from compulsive behavior can make possible—a sufficiency that comes from feeling you're in harmony with something greater than yourself. The men you've met so far are at the beginning of this journey, and every new step we accomplish takes effort, self-assessment, and what feels like "risk." Every new step takes us further away from the reflexive tactics, the guaranteed results we had developed so fearfully throughout our lives. This means the journey, as it progresses, is never easy. Every new "Aha!" moment—each new moment of insight—seems to be earned by passing through fear. But you have infinite help to overcome the fear, and a large part of that help comes from other people who are facing the same fears you are.

As I hope you'll see even more clearly in the next chapter, you can walk through the doorway with your hand held.

Chapter Five
"Only Connect"—Joining the Human Race

Becoming an adult human being seems to be a very different process than most of us were taught. There no longer seem to be obvious rites of passage to tell us we've hit the "grown-up" stage—actually, there never *have* been for gay men. For the better part of our history, we were barely acknowledged as human, much less capable of "growing up." Not for us the courtship/marriage/kids/home-in-the-burbs route: the touchstones of our progress have always been private and unique to our individual lives.

Compulsive gay men feel doubly outside the "norm." We confront the impossibility of ever becoming someone out of *The Brady Bunch* not only because we're *gay* but also because our compulsions set us so distantly apart. Compulsive gay men don't even feel they can be "nice" gay grown-ups. We seem to have a built-in sabotage mechanism that keeps screwing up any attempts we make to lead an "exemplary" life. It is the rare gay man who grows up feeling any visceral connection to a wider, "normal" community, but I doubt that there's ever been a compulsive gay man who didn't feel as if he were a small, lone asteroid in some other solar system. Isolation is the acid we've had to drink, had to pretend we could stomach and survive.

Compulsive gay men have the feeling of being different not only in the generic sense that gay people feel different from the heterosexual majority (which at least can make us feel like a small community of like-minded people), but also in a way that distances us even from other gay people. It can make you feel as if God hurriedly discarded *your* mold since it was so obviously defective. This feeling is so deeply rooted that it almost always persists to some degree even after your first recovery breakthrough. The moment the door to recovery opens is, as I hope we've seen, a wonderful, healing, life-changing experience, but moving into the new realm of recovery takes some additional effort and consciousness.

A word about recovery: what exactly are we trying to recover? Not, surely, the self we were the moment before we first acted out; that's the self that got us into the mess we've been trying to get out of! The sense of recovery my recovering compulsive friends are teaching me is quite different. What we want to recover is the capacity to grow, the capacity to become our best and freest selves—a capacity we had at birth. No wonder that we can't recover it perfectly or completely, but what a wonder it is to discover how much of it we can recover! So many compulsive people in Twelve Step programs call themselves "gratefully recovering" because they realize the enormous gift of the second chance they've been given to regain their capacity for life. We have the opportunity to develop an embracing attitude toward the world which people who don't need to grapple with these issues often never experience.

Recovery is a gift because it brings us to so much more than not acting out: it can open the door to realms beyond that. But it seems we can't begin to explore those realms until we recognize we are not *alone* in them. I had a lover once, years ago, who was literary; quoting E. M. Forster, he used to plead with me, "Only connect." "*Only connect* that your having all this anonymous sex and getting so drunk every night hurts me. Only connect to the idea that your actions do have consequences. You do have an impact on me—I'm not untouched." What my ex-lover didn't stick around long enough to say (I don't have a single ex-lover, by the way, who still talks to me, so you can imagine what a delight I was to be around) was that because I've got the power to act, the power to *affect* other people, I have an implicit responsibility to use that power consciously. However, before I can recognize that I have an impact on the world out there, I first have to accept that I'm a part of it—that I exist.

So many of us identify, I think, with what Matthew had to say in the last chapter: "I'd gone through the motions of life not really accepting that I was *alive*, that I was really there." Matthew couldn't believe it "when days or weeks or months later anyone would remember something I'd said or done. I couldn't accept that I'd actually had an impact on anything." My ex-lover and so many people after him kept assuring me I did have that impact, an impact of unwitting cruelty—a power to harm that I wielded most dangerously because I was almost completely unaware I had it. There is danger in self-hatred, not only to yourself but also to the people who love you. Not caring about yourself means not caring what you do—to anyone. It's no wonder we leave so many hurt people in our wake.

This is, and remains, an enormous, ongoing revelation: *I'm connected to other people.* So many of us, however, are so used to the acid of isolation and to thinking it's the only way we can survive that we resist any attempts to break through that isolation. Unfortunately, it doesn't seem possible to get sober in any sense without realizing your connection to the world. So much of what I'm learning about the meaning of sobriety is about being *conscious* of that connection—which translates, on one clear level at least, to people. The long and the short of it is, I need you guys out there. And if you're like the rest of us recovering compulsives, you need me too. Recovering that elusive capacity for growth seems inevitably to require opening our hearts to one another. There's no black-and-white goal, no gold star awarded to tell us that we've done this perfectly; connecting to other people is rarely like hitting a bull's-eye. We move *toward* greater closeness, and we are infinitely approachable—or so it seems to me, as I see no end to the depth and variety of communion that seems possible between me and other human beings, as long as I keep receptive. There is always room for more in our hearts—more love, more pain, more experience, more joy, more *people*. Discovering this can, initially, frighten us and intimidate us. It's awkward stuff, getting sober. It's awkward to change behavior you've clung to with all fours for most of your sentient life. "Anything a compulsive lets go of," I'm reminded at meetings again and again, "has claw marks all over it."

Releasing ourselves from isolation takes a kind of letting go we can't do only once—isolating is usually so reflexive that we've got to take steps every day to make sure we don't crawl back into the dark shadows we were used to. We've already heard that we don't get just one revelation and then stop. Recovery depends on continuing revelation, an ongoing scream of "Aha!" moments that have to do, most of them, with just this: *reconnecting ourselves to the universe.* I need to be continually gathered back into the fold. My compulsions continue to propel me away and out into the dark; my health depends on turning back toward the light until this turning becomes second nature, until I'm following a discipline of doing what I know will keep me sober. I wish I could say it got easier as you go along—in a sense it does, because you learn the rich rewards of connecting to the world, of improving your conscious contact with the universe (and other people). But the pain keeps cropping up, and life continues to bring us every crisis and emotion in the book. I was at a meeting once when someone who had more than thirty years of sobriety in AA said, "The only difference between me and someone with thirty days of sobriety is that I know it will pass." *It will pass.* The terrors and the anxieties and what seem to be inescapable conflicts: these will pass. But what aids your ability to tolerate their arrival, as well as prepare for their passing, is connecting to other people.

Here are some men who can help give a clearer idea of what I'm talking about.

THE DOOR TO FRIENDSHIP

Jeremy's story is so resonant because it reminds me, painfully, of how hard it's been to get used to having gay men as *friends* and how crucial it's been to develop that sense for my recovery. I don't think Jeremy and I are alone in this dilemma, which is why I offer his tale here.

Jeremy is a man you would imagine any number of other men falling in love with—and you'd be right. He has a heart-wrenching charm and wins you over instantly with his genuinely self-effacing, quiet humor—a slightly Jimmy Stewart "aw shucks" quality that is winning because it's so obviously not a ploy. Jeremy's self-effacement is all too real; unfortunately, it does not have positive roots. It grew from a lifetime of literally trying to efface himself (the dictionary definition: "blot out, erase"). The older son of two alcoholic parents, whose unpredictable flare-ups made him and his younger brother hide for safety throughout their childhood, Jeremy did as much as he could to appear inconspicuous. He's apologetic to a fault. ("When I bump into a chair I say I'm sorry," he only half jokes today, "to the chair.") Jeremy has not been entirely successful in effacing himself, however, because he's a big, tall, strapping man. As inconspicuous as he tries to be, his imposing physical presence marks him as someone special. It's a size and strength in which Jeremy takes secret, guilty pride—as if his animalness is out of his control and his attractiveness has a life of its own. Although he does everything to play down that attractiveness, Jeremy knows he draws people to him, and it's a source of conflict, a pull between guilty pleasure in attracting attention and a deeply rooted sense that he's unworthy of any attention to all.

Jeremy developed a fixation on men's room sex that seemed to emblematize this conflict—it was a way for him to be noticed in a way that would also make him feel guilty. His sense of himself as worthless was reinforced by the "demeaning" sexual venue; his desire to be "adored" was, however, given vent as well. He remembers the first time "it" happened: "I had a college interview, which was to be held in this old hotel, I was seventeen. I was nervous, and I got there early and had to pee. I found the men's room, which was one of those old, huge, white-tiled Edwardian affairs with huge porcelain urinals. Only one other man, an older guy in his late thirties, I guess, was there. I took my place a few urinals down from him, not especially aware of him. Not aware, that is, until I saw him step back a little to reveal his erect penis. It was terrifying. Nobody had ever exposed himself to me before, and I didn't know what he might do to me or if I was safe, but I was riveted too. I didn't move—I stared down at my own feet. He zipped up temporarily and then moved down to the urinal next to me. Then, without a word, he got down on his knees. I was scared to death. It was the first time I'd ever had any kind of sex with anybody, but something secret in me rejoiced. The shame and the release—I know now that I was a men's room freak just waiting to happen."

Jeremy's story somewhat parallels Matthew's: he would slink away to men's rooms every chance he could get. It became an addiction over the years that took hours out of each day. He remembers sitting on one particular toilet for seven hours straight, waiting that whole time for "the right man" to walk in and service him. Over the years his self-esteem leaked away, as if into all those toilets, to the point where he couldn't look anyone he knew in the eye. What people read as self-effacing charm was really a mirror of how ashamed Jeremy felt of himself. He kept looking down at his feet, not in some shy ruse designed to appeal but because he was steeped in a deep self-loathing—one so deep as to be barely conscious. But the "charm" worked nevertheless. Jeremy attracted a number of lovers, lovers who, when they inevitably found out what Jeremy did with hours of each day, were heartbroken by his "sordid" betrayals. Abject love of Jeremy eventually turned, with each man, into abject disgust.

Jeremy's misery increased to the point where he knew he had to do something. He didn't define himself as sexually compulsive—he didn't know there was such a thing, at first—but someone suggested he look into Adult Children of Alcoholics (ACOA). ACOA was wonderful: Jeremy felt the ready understanding and rush of identification we've seen in

Matthew, Grant, and Peter. But his men's room habit didn't abate. He was getting a glimmer of what recovery might mean—a glimmer of possibility that perhaps he had a choice not to hate himself or do hateful things *to* himself. But it wasn't until he discovered Sexual Compulsives Anonymous (SCA) that he began to realize the full extent of his self-loathing. Jeremy has had a difficult time coming to terms with this (who doesn't have a hard time facing up to self-hate?), but some of his difficulties stemmed from his being baffled at how to behave with men in the program who merely wanted to *talk*—to share and help and be helped in recovery. He started to go out to coffee with people after meetings, but he'd sit across from whoever it was who had asked him out and try to keep from squirming with discomfort. How was he supposed to react? He realized he'd never spent time with another man when it hadn't led to sex. It was totally beyond him simply to *be* with another man, especially an attractive gay man, and allow that simple encounter to be sufficient. Invariably, after talking with someone from the program, he'd feel the overwhelming urge to act out. It was as if he had to take the feelings that had begun in "innocence" and turn them into something familiar and self-abusive: "lust."

It was tearing him apart. As much as other men in SCA said things about their own struggles to be sexually sober with which he could identify, he always held a part of himself back. He couldn't help feeling a "Yes, but. . . ." ("Yes, but you're still not *me*. You don't know what it's like to be me. I'm still different from you.")

One night, Jeremy's phone rang. He sleepily looked at the clock. It was after 2:00 in the morning. Who would be calling him this late? He answered angrily and heard a sobbing voice. "Look, Jeremy," the voice said, "I'm sorry, but I really need . . ." and the voice disintegrated again into tears. Jeremy was able to figure out who it was—a man with whom he'd had coffee two nights before, following an SCA meeting. He was someone with whom Jeremy had felt especially awkward, someone Jeremy was now very surprised would be calling for help. He tried to listen. He found himself saying reassuring, gentle, helpful things: "It's all right, whatever it is, it'll be all right." The man on the other end of the phone began to calm down. He said how he'd just gotten in from a subway men's room where he'd spent all night. Some guy had beaten him up. He was afraid maybe a rib was broken. He didn't know who to turn to. Could Jeremy, maybe, meet him and go with him to the emergency room? He couldn't go to the police because they'd ask him what he'd been doing in the men's room at that hour. He couldn't risk the exposure—he was a teacher, he would lose his job. He thought maybe he'd lost a lot of blood. He was a mess, he had no one to turn to. . . .

Jeremy groaned inwardly—a complicated groan of sympathy for the guy and a *profound* resistance to getting up at 2:30 A.M. to help him. This wasn't what Jeremy knew how to do. It was totally alien to him to be called by someone in this much need, and yet something propelled Jeremy to say yes, to continue his reassurances that things would be okay, to tell the man he'd be over in a few minutes. Jeremy pulled on some clothes, flagged down a cab, and got to the man's apartment within the half hour.

The guy, eyes wide and frightened, a face swollen and streaked with dried blood, shaking like a leaf, softly whimpering in pain from what was obviously a brutal beating, apologized profusely to Jeremy. Half-coherent, he went over what happened, how he didn't know anybody to call, how he had no friends, and he saw Jeremy's number and didn't know what else to do. . . .

Jeremy saw him through the indignities of a late-night city hospital emergency room, holding his hand (Holding his hand! Jeremy thought. He'd never done anything so flagrantly "gay" before—at least not out of a men's room), taking care of documents and red tape, seeing the guy through the whole ordeal. When the man was finally dealt with, wrapped and bandaged and allowed to go home, it was 6:00 in the morning and the sky was getting light. Jeremy had long since stopped feeling awkward; he'd discovered resources in himself he never knew existed. He had done what had to be done. He delivered the man home, helped to undress him, tucked him in, and said he'd call later that day.

This contact—this raw contact, as raw as sex but somehow satisfying in a way sex never had been—was baffling to Jeremy. He was thrust into a situation of helping another gay man where there was nothing ambiguous about what had to be done. There was no question of sexual innuendo, no question of anything but responding to the man's need, simply and fully. It was the first time Jeremy had felt this. It began to dawn on him that there might be other kinds of contacts between men—between gay men—than he realized there could be. He called the man, as he promised he would, and went over later that afternoon with soup and pie. Every new act amazed him: he was actually *helping* somebody.

Jeremy often talks about the awakening this meant. It was such a new experience for him: "It made me think of myself, myself as a gay man, differently. I'd always thought of myself as basically less than human—a rampaging male instinct barely held in, held in with only the greatest constraints—

and capable of nothing with another man that didn't involve raw sex or abject apology. To help another man because you wanted to help, because you knew help was needed—this was a whole new ball game. And it's begun to get me to look at myself differently, to value myself and what it might mean to be a 'gay man,' more than I ever thought I could."

The nature of the trouble his beaten-up friend had gotten into wasn't lost on Jeremy either: "It was obvious now that I wasn't the only guy tortured by men's room sex. What happened to that guy could just as easily have happened to me. Somehow, until that moment, I hadn't really believed anyone else was as compulsive as I was—in the same ways I was. Now there was no doubt. I wasn't alone."

"I wasn't alone." The door to friendship opened for Jeremy, and the suggestion that he might be able to be with someone for reasons other than mere sex alternately baffles and elates him. "I have a whole new area to cultivate—friendships with other people. And it's okay that I'm awkward at it. Everyone is awkward at it! I'm so struck by the irony of a whole group of men—men who, each of them, felt totally separate and isolated and alone—now forming a *group*, doing what they'd thought was impossible: listening, talking, sharing, helping. These are not just abstract words to me now. I'm learning what they feel like—what it's like to actually live them."

Because they're so alien, what these new behaviors and emotions "feel like" is, sometimes, frightening. But organically, just through the experience of having opened himself to a new kind of communion with other gay men, Jeremy is discovering that his urge to act out sexually has begun to abate, to lift. There is no direct cause and effect that he can point to, unless it's the fact that he spontaneously finds he doesn't hate himself as much as he used to, and thus doesn't seem to need to prove to himself that he's hateful by acting out in ways he knows will depress him. As I hope we've seen with the other men we've talked about, this "lifting" of the urge to act out isn't something that just happens once and for all—it takes continual vigilance to get back to the sense of elation and possibility that Jeremy feels at the best of times. But he doesn't just have to remind himself: he can—and he's discovering now that he needs to—turn to other recovering compulsive people for those reminders. He's accepted a very important truth about his compulsive confreres: they understand what he's going through.

Jeremy allowed himself to open up to the idea that his confreres *could* understand what he was going through by making a strongly felt but, amazing to him, nonsexual connection to one of them. He helped somebody. That experience of helping other people is so much more surprising than most of us expect it to be. It's no wonder we tend to glaze over at platitudes such as "It's better to give than to receive"; it's difficult to talk about the joy that comes from reaching out without sounding like a church pamphlet. But the joy is so great, it allows such an extraordinary feeling of bonding to other people, that it deserves to be explored from this side of the pulpit.

FACING A GROUP

Mark's terrible feeling of isolation is, again, familiar to most of us. Like Jeremy, he is the survivor of an alcoholic family. His terrifyingly brutal and unpredictable father would haul off and hit him for no reason. Mark grew up in a thick atmosphere of fear and was driven into himself, shut off from other people. He didn't dare invite home any of the few friends he managed to acquire—he never knew when his father would blow up. Mark says he realized he was gay when he was twelve; it was a very vivid moment. His father was watching professional wrestling on TV, and Mark stood by the door to the kitchen at the other end of the living room, trying, as always, to be as inconspicuous as possible, but he was suddenly riveted by the huge half-naked men throwing each other around on the screen. He got an erection. Something about the *beating* was unimaginably, shamefully, exciting.

It's no surprise that Mark eroticized his fear and rage—that he was attracted to sadomasochism. His father had all but brought him up to be a masochist. But the masochistic role Mark felt compelled to play in the sexual relationships he eventually got into—compulsively, as he moved to a big city where he could connect easily with other men into S&M—never fully satisfied him. He always ended in self-hate, which always reinforced his sense of feeling like shit. He couldn't imagine sharing this dark self with anyone, even after he heard of the existence of some self-help groups that appeared to be tailor-made for him. Like Jeremy, he began going to gay ACOA meetings, and then went to some SCA meetings as well. He knew he was in the right ballpark, but his self-hatred was so strong that it became a real obstacle to identifying fully with anyone he heard. And the few times he got the courage to raise his hand in meetings, no one ever called on him. He began to feel he was being singled out, that he was a Twelve Step pariah. He had only to walk into a Twelve Step meeting to be ignored. He imagined someone had put a hex on him. He imagined, not only in meetings but also when he walked down the street, that people automatically disliked him, automatically avoided him. And his recourse was to seek out more s&m sex, in more and more abused masochistic roles. He lived and breathed self-hatred.

One evening, at the end of an sca meeting when, again, no one had called on him and Mark was feeling his usual abysmal depression, the chairman announced that he wouldn't be able to be there the following week and asked if somebody would please volunteer to take over the meeting for him. No one raised his hand. The chairman's eyes scanned the room and settled, for some reason, on Mark. "What about you?" He smiled at him. "You're always at meetings—you know what goes on." At first, Mark couldn't believe the guy was address-ing him. He wanted to say no, but he couldn't croak the word out. What came out sounded suspiciously like "okay." The chairman thanked him and asked to talk to him after the meeting to fill him in on a few details.

Mark clenched during the Serenity Prayer, with which the meeting always closed. He remembers feeling almost attacked by its words—not the usual peace (or at least bland comfort) he'd felt when he'd heard the prayer before. *God grant me the serenity* (I can't chair the meeting! Mark thought to himself.) *to accept the things I cannot change* (Well, I certainly don't have to accept this—I'll just back out when I talk to the chairman.) *the courage to change the things I can* (That lets me out since I haven't got any courage.) *and the wisdom to know the differ-ence.* Something hit Mark at the mention of "wisdom." He'd never "heard" such a tortured Serenity Prayer, but suddenly he knew he'd go through with it; he'd keep his agreement to take over the meeting. He didn't want to, but he'd do it.

Nightmares about the upcoming evening plagued him throughout the intervening days, and more than once he reached to dial the number he'd been given in case there was an emergency and he had to back out. The thought of saying anything in front of a group was frightening enough (Why did I ever want to get called on, anyway? Mark thought. I'd just make a fool of myself!), but the thought of *leading* a group was paralyzing. Somehow, Mark didn't bail out.

Nerves made him get to the meeting room an hour early. He knew he'd be alone, but he'd forgotten that there would be no one to help him pull out the sixty or seventy folding chairs from the basement closet and then set them up. It seemed like an impossible task, and he tried pulling out four or five at a time. He nearly squashed a finger on the second haul, so, reluctantly, he kept himself to two chairs a trip. He felt anxious. He flashed back to mowing the lawn as a kid. His father, drunk and abusive, would time him, and if he wasn't done in whatever the allotted time was, he'd get slapped. He remembered how it seemed there was always so much more lawn to go. That's what he felt with these chairs, or, at least, it's what he felt until, slowly, he began to see a horseshoe pattern of chairs forming in the room.

Then he had a wonderful insight: *he* was creating that pattern!

It seemed a simple—even a silly—thing, but somehow it amazed him, even elated him. How many meetings had he been to without realizing that someone had had to set up the chairs? He looked at the room as it began to transform into a meeting place, and he was astounded at the inescapable fact that *he* was doing it. He had more than half the chairs set up by the time the first people trickled in. A few helped him drag out the remaining chairs. One of them asked him, "You chairing the meeting?" When Mark said he was, the man smiled warmly and said "Good!" Why did this exchange mean so much to him? He felt suffused with something very close to happiness.

Mark began the meeting a little nervously but then fell into stride. ("I kept looking at how orderly all the chairs were!") He read the opening statement for Sexual Compulsives Anonymous, asked if anyone was new to the meeting and wanted to introduce himself by first name, asked if anyone was counting days or having an anniversary he wanted to share. With each of his chairman duties, he gained confidence, marveling inwardly that he was *contributing* something, marveling at the wonderful sense of well-being it gave him. It was what he felt when he saw himself create a pattern in the room—a delighted "I did this!" He suddenly realized he'd totally forgotten to be nervous.

The hour went by smoothly, and as Mark led the group in the Serenity Prayer, he found himself embracing—and understanding—the words more deeply than ever before. He wasn't fighting them the way he had the previous week. After the meeting, several men walked up to him, complimented him on a nice job, and asked him out to coffee. "The strange thing was," Mark sums up, "what I'd always wanted to have happen—to be accepted as a member of a group— was happening without any of the *effort* I was sure it had to take. All I'd done was a few simple chairman tasks, but I'd never felt more connected. It's not that some Pollyanna transformation happened to get rid of my sexual compulsion, but I didn't have that terrible gut feeling anymore that nobody could really understand. I thought now that maybe they could. And somehow this all started because I set up a bunch of chairs at a meeting. I began to understand the meaning of a phrase I kept hearing at meetings; I understood what it means just to 'show up' and let God do the rest."

Again, it's difficult to talk about this without sounding simplistic, as if there's always some instant, magical cause-and-effect relationship between "doing good" and "getting better." Set up some chairs and watch your troubles disappear (and whistle while you work). But, again, nothing quite prepares you for the serenity and well-being most of us end up feeling when we do what Twelve Step programs call "service." It works. You feel connected, purposeful, a part of things. Mark says that feeling of purpose and connection was once so foreign to him that he had long ago given up hope it could be part of his life. But his chairmanship experience was a revelation. Now he's volunteered to do hospitality in his ACOA meeting, which means he makes the coffee, gets the cookies, and (his favorite part!) helps set up chairs. "Hell," he says, "I'd do basket weaving if I thought it would help." Help who? He points to the people who are milling around the coffee urn and sitting down in a semicircle: "Them—and me."

The effect of "service" on compulsivity is not guaranteed. The effect of anything on compulsivity, my friends tell me, isn't guaranteed—except for one thing. If you don't act out, you won't suffer the consequences of acting out (for example, you can't get drunk if you don't drink). But there seems to be a marvelous effect on self-esteem from contributing service, from doing something for more than just yourself. Problems with self-esteem, as we've already seen, are at the root of all the bumps in our rugs. When we increase that esteem in ways that last, we don't seem to need to act out with quite the old urgency, or so people wiser than I keep telling me and showing me by their own example.

Connecting one-to-one, and service to a group of people, can have so many benefits, but because it seems that you begin to reap those benefits not by hearing about them but by reaching out yourself to connect, maybe we don't need to say more. Equally important, however, is allowing yourself to be reached. Equally important is to develop trust that other people want to help you—to contribute to *your* sobriety. The capacity to receive help seems to be as important as the capacity to give it, as Bruno, in our next story, will show us.

HEARING AND BEING HEARD

Bruno vibrates with nervous energy. Partially, it's his background: he says he's the product of two volatile parents, one Italian, the other Polish, who met in Vienna, where each had gone to university in their mid-thirties, just as it was becoming wise to get *out* of Austria and Germany if you were Jewish. Both Bruno's parents were Jewish, but they stayed in Vienna until the very end of the decade—long enough to get married and have an infant son, Bruno, and long enough so that they had to smuggle themselves out with expensively obtained false passports in 1939. Bruno was three years old and remembers a little about their escape: the loud noise of a locomotive, the smells of a crowded station, the vague sight of buildings, clouds, people rushing by, and the overriding feeling that he wasn't safe.

When Bruno's family got to America, all but penniless, and found their way to Chicago, Bruno's feeling that he wasn't safe did not improve. Rumors filtered in to the family that their relatives were being rounded up and sent to concentration camps, and though he was too young to understand what was going on at the time, Bruno was not too young to absorb his parents' terror, pain, and grief. He also remembers from his earliest childhood in Chicago that he never once felt really taken care of. "They curtained off a section of one of the two rooms of our apartment for me," Bruno says. "We were very poor and they couldn't afford any better. But I heard my parents fight day and night, long after they'd put me to bed. Once they were making so much noise, sounding so violent, that—I must have been about five—I toddled out from behind the curtain to plead with them to stop." Bruno caught his mother and father in flagrant delicto. He didn't understand that they were "making love"; he thought his father was attacking his mother. He screamed, and couldn't stop screaming. His father, naked, leapt out of bed and swatted him across the face, shoving him back through the curtain into his corner of the room, shouting at him never to come out again.

Bruno realizes this is almost too classic an episode. "I've been through so much therapy in my life," he says, "that I'm almost embarrassed that I've got such a textbook case about the Oedipal conflict!" he jokes. But the shock was real. And the wariness of his parents is something that has plagued him ever since. He took his father's order "never to come out again" sadly to heart; he felt severed and withdrawn from that moment on.

Bruno was also plagued by an insatiable desire for food. He was always hungry. "Mama must have felt guilty about how Papa treated me—I don't know—but although she never really said a kind word to me, she did feed me. She was the Italian one, so that meant hills of pasta, meatballs, bread." By the time he was twelve, Bruno topped 190 pounds. By the time he was sixteen, he'd passed 250 pounds.

The only attention he ever got from his parents (and,

because she was the one who did the cooking, this really only meant his mother) was food. Bruno has been through enough analysis to see some clear reasons for his compulsive overeating—food to him was love—and now he has a good idea why he had another compulsion. He couldn't stop talking. "When I finally got out of the house," which Bruno says he did at age of eighteen, the day after high school graduation, "I found myself a room at the YMCA and got a job in a gay restaurant as a cook." He says his huge girth seemed to qualify him for the job as much as anything else ("the manager assumed I knew something about food"). But Bruno says he was fired within a month not because he wasn't a good cook (he was: he'd watched Mama very carefully) but because he wouldn't shut up. "I simply wouldn't stop jabbering to the kitchen help," Bruno says. "I know I kept up this motormouth commentary on everything because it felt like the first time I was able to talk." Every time Bruno had opened his mouth at home—unless it was opened to eat—he was either told to shut up or was simply ignored. He had a deep-rooted sense that nobody wanted to listen to him.

Bruno had a series of dishwasher and short-order cook jobs, losing them because he could never get along with anyone on the job. ("I used to fantasize my tombstone would say something like You Got Your Way at Last. Bruno Finally Shut Up.'") His only "relationships" happened—infrequently—in the shower room of the YMCA where he still lived. He would turn on the water and stand under it, waiting for the sound of the shower to attract somebody—somebody who might put up with getting sexually serviced by a fat man. These were his only "intimate" contacts, and they didn't happen often.

It was his loneliness as much as his overeating that drove

him, years later, to Overeaters Anonymous. In a desperate attempt to be accepted, Bruno threw himself into the program—and it *did* begin to work for him. He did become conscious of his powerlessness over food. He understood that the Twelve Step approach could help him, and he began to lose weight and feel marginally better about himself. But what he couldn't stop doing was *talking.*

Alas, as forbearing and understanding and loving as most people in Twelve Step programs are, we are also a breed peculiarly sensitive to the "injustice" of somebody hogging the stage. One recovering compulsive friend of mine tries to check himself about what he calls his own arrogance: "No wonder I get so mad at people who, obliviously, go on and on at meetings. It bothers the hell out of me because that's exactly what *I* did when I was drunk." It's the old truth that we don't like in other people what we are afraid of being ourselves—and it's a useful truth. But, alas for poor Bruno, he engendered some strong resentments wherever he went—including Twelve Step meetings. Then, thank heavens (for him and everyone else), he had a breakthrough. As with all the breakthroughs we've talked about in this book, it was deceptively simple.

He found himself in a particularly long rant in the middle of an OA meeting when something made him come out of himself. "Actually," Bruno says, "the chairman sneezed. I looked up at him, wiping his nose, and for some reason seeing him do that simple action made something click. *He* existed too. The guy who sneezed was just as important as I was." Bruno paused in the middle of his usual filibuster to notice something else: "People in the room were looking at me expectantly, waiting for me to continue. They were actually *listening.* It was phenomenal." Bruno says he felt tears well up. He said to the group, "I don't have to keep talking, do I?

You're not going to tell me to shut up the way I was always told to shut up as a kid. You're not judging me. You're *listening*. . . ."

Bruno felt an enormous knot of anxiety loosen. "It was as if every fiber in me began to relax. I felt this huge surge of trust." For the first time he could remember, people who spoke later in the meeting thanked him for what he said—thanked him for helping *them!*

A curious paradox of recovery seems to be that we can help other people, sometimes, by showing that we need help—that we are receptive. We can help others to open up by being open ourselves. Everything seems to work by "power of example" (show-and-tell, with the emphasis on show). A wonderful dividend for Bruno has been his own increased ability to listen. It is a pleasure and an adventure that he says he had never allowed himself before. "Once I could accept that I didn't have to monopolize every conversation to be heard, I could begin to listen to other people as well. What a miracle it is to actually *let someone finish a sentence!* I never knew how much I interrupted people until I made myself do a little experiment: I allowed someone to talk until he was done."

The peace this can lead to is wonderful. Bruno calls it "acceptance in action. I don't feel, anymore, that I've got to cram everything I think and feel into one breath. Now I try to give myself permission to breathe—to hold back when I'm not clear yet about what I think. And what other people have to say now seems like such a gift. I now experience people from start to finish—and how much more they have to say than I ever thought they did!"

I've never met a compulsive gay man who didn't start by

feeling he was in his own orbit. What people like Bruno, Mark, and Jeremy teach me is that we are in a galaxy of similar planets, and that it's by recognizing and allowing ourselves to enjoy our connections to others that amazing things can happen. Sometimes it seems we "recover" only as far as we recover a sense of unity with other people. I've had this demonstrated to me every day of my life—every day I go to a Twelve Step meeting.

"Dr. Bob," the co-founder with Bill Wilson of AA, neatly summed up what he felt the Twelve Steps amounted to in two words: "love and service." Perhaps that's the point of all we've been exploring: to turn those nouns into verbs and then to live by them seems crucial to recovering from any compulsion. A feeling of joy and serenity seems to be the inescapable dividend.

Chapter Six
*Going Too F-A-R: Dealing with Fear, Anger, and Resentment
(And All the Other Feelings You Think Will Kill You)*

This is still embarrassing for me to admit—which means I'm
still working on it—but I can't stand the sound of someone
chewing. It's been this way as far back as I can recall. I
remember stomping away in a fury from the little girl who
was my neighbor and playmate when both of us were five.
She was eating a peanut butter and jelly sandwich, and the
sound of it mucking about in her mouth made me want
to . . . Can a five-year-old want to *kill?* Up until recently,
when I couldn't find another seat far, far across the room,
I've been known to storm out of a diner at the sound of
someone innocently (but noisily) making his way through a
meal. I feel like a nut case, but I can't help it. It makes me
want to climb the walls. Or worse.

The point of this confession isn't to throw some interesting
psychological neurosis up for analysis (although I'm always
in the market for insights about it!). The point, for me, is to
remind myself of how strong, involuntary, deep-rooted, irra-
tional, and devastating feelings can be. Emotions can be like
lit matches near gasoline—the whole mess can explode in an

instant, blotting out everything in a sudden blast. What gets talked about in Twelve Step meetings more, perhaps, than anything else is how to *deal* with these uncomfortable feelings and, more specifically, how to keep from resorting to our compulsive escape hatches when it seems as if we can't tolerate what we feel.

I've coined the acronym F-A-R to sum up what seem to be three of the most devastating—and dangerous—feelings people, and especially compulsive people, have to deal with: fear, anger, and resentment. The first two of these, fear and anger, are so reflexive, so deeply inbred that they've hit us before we know it. If psychologists are right, it's no wonder we have no power over them: the fight-or-flight instinct, which seems to be programmed into every animal on the face of the earth, is programmed into us too. "Fight" (anger) and "flight" (fear) seem to be responses as primal as sleeping when we're tired or eating when we're hungry. Thus, accepting the inevitability of feeling fear or anger seems to be the first step in dealing with them.

I'm not sure why I welcome this self-evident truth so strongly. I suppose it's that, like so many other people, I've been convinced all of my life that fear and anger or, for that matter, any emotion I feel, are my doing—my *fault*. That if I were the saint, the angel, the perfectly evolved transcendent being I'm "supposed" to be, I wouldn't be plagued by anything so wretched as a human feeling—especially ones as base and destructive as fear or anger. Compulsive people tend to feel guilty about everything in their lives—when they aren't blaming someone or something else for what's going wrong. What Twelve Step recovery seems to teach us is that this whole notion of *blaming*—whether ourselves or somebody else—has to go. We can't recover with that perspective. We have to start, first, by becoming aware of what we are feeling—then we have to accept it. Only then might we be in a position to act in a positive way. I hear in meetings that these are the three *A*s of AA: awareness, acceptance, and action. You can't get to the second *A* without experiencing the first, nor the third without experiencing the second.

Okay. I'm aware I can't stand the sound of chewing. And I'm even willing to accept that this is a reflex feeling I can't seem to avoid. But what happens the next time I'm in a diner and the sweet old lady in the next booth slurps into her oatmeal? *Whammo.* Before I've even thought of the Serenity Prayer, my emotions have zapped in like a sudden thunderstorm.

Something tells me you can relate to this. You're walking behind three slow-moving human beings who are blocking the entire sidewalk (the idea of a submachine gun occurs). You've ordered decaf coffee and you watch the sullen guy behind the counter deliberately reach for the regular coffee (you wish you had a hand grenade). Your lover has again forgotten to (choose one): take the laundry, screw the cap back on the toothpaste, feed the cat, water the plants (you try to remember the name of that palimony lawyer). The list goes on, and if you're not going through the experience, it can look like a pretty trivial list. Grist for the mills of tired sitcoms or advice columns. But these daily annoyances are some of the most dangerous triggers compulsive people face. Many of us thrive on "crises"—our attraction to high drama makes us, often, very good at responding to the Big Moments in Life. It's the day-to-day stuff that can put us under.

Again, this would only be moderately interesting if it weren't so dangerous. Feelings—and not only "negative" feelings like fear, anger, resentment, depression, and grief but also "positive" feelings like joy, excitement, triumph, and love—are what usually "send us out": back to food, sex, booze, drugs, and unhealthy relationships. Nothing triggers the compulsive urge like the stimulus of a powerful feeling. To have any chance of lasting sobriety or serenity, it seems to be crucial to work out ways to deal with the sudden onslaught of our emotions.

Alcoholics Anonymous's Big Book tells us that resentment is the number one offender—the first feeling we must look at if we want to hold on to sobriety. It seems to be different from fear and anger in one crucial respect: we *manufacture* it; we are not simply *hit* by it. Human beings are the only mammals on earth who feel resentment; it is one of the traits that sets us apart. Resentment, unlike fear or anger, seems to be something we make and, sometimes, hold on to for what would seem to other mammals to be some pretty peculiar payoffs.

The idea that we manufacture resentment doesn't mean that resentment can't feel every bit as unavoidable as fear or anger; it's not that it doesn't hit us in the same primal, unconscious way. When your boss makes some snide remark about your work, when someone says you're fat, when you feel you are unjustly accused of this or that wrongdoing, the feeling of resentment can hit every bit as powerfully and quickly as fear or anger. If we manufacture it, then we do it in an instant—unconsciously. But accepting that we manufacture it invites us to look at what we make it *out* of. It invites us to look at our motives for creating our resentments.

Resentment always seems to hide something more basic. We make our resentments in response to something primal: we seem to feel a resentment against anyone or anything that threatens to *deprive* us. What alcoholic, while he's still drinking, doesn't resent being around people who don't drink? What sex addict feels at ease in an AIDS clinic? What workaholic enjoys the prospect of a leisurely vacation? What compulsive overeater really likes Weight Watchers celeb-of-the-month commercials?

Just this short list of questions is enough to indicate how quick and self-protective our resentments can be—how clearly they happen because we feel *threatened.* They suggest a natural progression in our acronym F-A-R: fear leads to anger leads to resentment. When you snatch away a baby's pacifier, he'll respond first in fear (you've taken something away that he *depends* on), then in anger ("Give it back, *now!*"), then, if you do it often enough, in resentment ("Here comes that big person again who always makes me feel so awful!"). We may wonder that the infant screams bloody murder, but if we could enter into the baby's mind, we would feel his life-or-death urgency and we'd understand. If we've already seen that compulsive people are ingenious connivers at holding on to their denial—and their ways to act out—we shouldn't be surprised that we're capable of such raging resentments and paralyzing fears. We've gone through our lives reflexively resisting what we perceive to be attack, just like that baby deprived of his pacifier: it feels like a threat that something very dear to us will be snatched away. That reflex dies hard. But it seems to be a reflex we have got to look at if we are to live any kind of satisfying life in sobriety.

THE FEAR OF BEING DEPRIVED

The bad news, my friend Rick tells me, is "there is no real equivalent to eating an entire Entenmann's raspberry coffee cake. There is no precise equivalent for six shots of Stolichnaya. There is no precise equivalent for four hours of hot, unbridled sex with five men in the baths. Nothing else will make you, even remotely, *feel* the same way." Rick knows whereof he speaks: he once got the only satisfaction he felt capable of getting from that list of compulsive activities. And he's banged his head against numerous brick walls in the attempt to match his "vices" with harmless but adequate replacements. "I think this is why so many people don't get Twelve Step programs," he says. "Their main question always seems to be: 'But what am I supposed to do *instead*?' It's not that that's a bad question," Rick says, "it's just that they've already decided what the answer has to be. Nothing can replace instant gratification except instant gratification of another kind. It's the whole diet mentality of 'fill up until you burst' on celery instead of potato chips. Unfortunately, celery makes a pretty poor substitute for potato chips, so you just go back to what works—the chips."

The problem comes when we define "what works" in terms of the thing we are trying to replace. That's the kind of (lunatic) expectation compulsive people who don't get the program seem to keep having: desperately trying quick fixes doomed to be inadequate because they can't replace what was already doing a terrific job. (Club soda instead of a vodka tonic? Who's kidding whom?)

Rick defines himself as a battle-scarred veteran of the search for a quick fix. "And of course," he says, "I was going to resent the hell out of anybody who threatened to deprive me of what I knew would work." Anger and resentment were a kind of fuel—they kept him, in a sense, on track— the track back to his addiction. And as such they were very useful emotions: they made sure he kept acting out. "I was like Pavlov's dog: the first hint of anger and I reached for a drink; the first welling-up of resentment at my lover or my boss and I was off to the baths. My feeling was 'I'll show them.'"

Feelings don't have to be "bad" to trigger the urge to act out. Remember Peter, back in chapter 4, when, flush with wonderful feelings about his alcoholic sobriety, he sought someone to have sex with as quickly as he could? It may have surprised him to hear it then, but he was trying to get *out of* his feeling of elation. He felt he couldn't contain that much stimulation. We can react as compulsively to "good" feelings as we do to "bad." Rick says that feeling elated was, often, an even bigger inducement to act out. "I guess I didn't really feel I deserved to feel good," he says. "I was so afraid the feeling would pass that I tried to set it in amber to make sure it *didn't go away.* That's what pigging out on sex, booze, or food seemed to do, at least at the beginning. But the real function of acting out was to turn what had started out as 'happiness' back into something I was more familiar with. Acting out would dull the intensity so that I could achieve a comfortable zombie state where nothing would matter anymore. Then, of course, when I came down from the high, when I awoke from that inertia, I'd be back to the old self-loathing—right where I started, right where I guess I really thought I deserved to be."

Acting out is eventual poison to "good" feelings and fuel to "bad" ones. "When I acted out," Rick says, "it was always like putting myself through a wringer. I was completely flattened out at the end, no matter what shape I started out."

"GET ME OUT OF MYSELF—I CAN'T STAND IT IN HERE!"

When we react to feelings in the Pavlovian way Rick describes, when we treat the realm of our feelings like some kind of hot pan we have to keep jumping out of not to get burned, we are obviously trapped. As long as we hold on to this fear of our own emotions, we've got no choice but to jump around in that scalding pan. We can do nothing but react—blindly, involuntarily, unthinkingly. However, given the alternatives we've set up for ourselves out of fear, it's no wonder we seek release. We feel we'd jump out of our *skins* otherwise. Please, we silently plead with our drug contact or God or the bartender, get me out of myself. I can't stand it in here!

As we've seen before, as long as we agree to submit to the tug-of-war between acting out and fear, it's no secret which side will win. And, as we've also seen, as long as we define satisfaction solely in terms of *instant* removal from our feelings, nothing will work for us *but* quick fixes. We've set it up that way. Of course, after a while, not even quick fixes work anymore. Or they work so "well," if what we want them to do is numb us out, that we are numbed out permanently—they kill us. Something else has to be done about feelings than what we've been doing. The answer seems to be to open our eyes to the general state that's causing us to snap away from any emotion we have. We have to look at what we think we're so afraid of.

You can be sober in an alcoholic, drug, food, sex, or any other sense for years and still recoil at the thought of facing fear. As suggested earlier, we are programmed as animals to react in fear or anger; it's an inescapable part of our makeup, and there's no way to avoid those "fight or flight" instincts, but there are ways to keep from reacting self-destructively and ways to keep those primal emotions from turning into resentment and acting-out behavior.

A man named Brian, with four years of what he calls "hard-won sobriety" in AA, gives us an example of how he was able to shift his perspective about fear—how he's become able to distance himself in order to see it—so that he can give himself time to choose how to react. "But what a task!" he says. "If I'm blessed with a long life in sobriety, I can imagine saying toward the end of it, 'Boy, those first twenty years were a *bitch!*'

"Don't let that discourage anybody who's new, though. Life is a hell of a lot better—even with the difficulties of dealing with my feelings sober—than it ever was when I drank. But, oh, mama never told me it would be like this." Being sober, says Brian, "is a matter of returning to infancy, where everything is new again. It's like that biblical story about Adam getting to name all the animals in the world. That's what I feel I've had to do too—name everything all over again. Especially my feelings. Frankly, when I drank, I never knew I had any." Brian pauses and emends: "That's not strictly true. I knew fear—briefly. I became so skilled at blotting out fear with booze that it seemed I never felt it for more than an instant. And I knew anger—boy, did I know it. Booze allowed me to blow up with what felt like full conviction. As Norman Maine said in *A Star Is Born,* 'I break up things, places, and people.' I also got thrown out of a lot of bars. But the *release.* It felt so good until, afterward, I pieced together what I'd done, what I'd destroyed. I was completely out of control."

When Brian got sober in AA his anger was still a problem. His sponsor kept reminding him that he probably would feel vulnerable—new and raw—and defenseless without alcohol. And that he could depend on him and other people in the program to help him through. But Brian couldn't deal with people *not* in the program. He started blowing up at his boss and losing his temper on a weekly basis, totally baffling everyone he worked with. They'd never seen him like this! ("Of course they hadn't," Brian says. "I'd always saved my rage for when I got drunk after work.") Brian's boss threatened to fire him after one particularly violent blowup, and Brian nearly lost a client in the food-catering business where he worked, a business whose pressures had never bothered Brian to this degree before. "I lost anything resembling tact," he says. "I was out of control."

That all this was happening in sobriety was especially distressing. Brian couldn't figure out what was wrong or forgive himself. He'd go to meetings, read the Big Book, try to meditate to calm down, and he'd be okay. Then somebody would cross him and he'd lose it. Once, after an explosion, he ran out of his office, out of the building, and into a park. He'd never just left like that before. He sank down on a bench, put his head in his hands, and cried. A very clear feeling came up—the terribly painful acknowledgment of grief. "It was as if someone had died," Brian said. "And then I began to realize that someone had. The old me—the drinking me. I began to accept in that moment that I no longer had the crutch I'd spent so many years depending on. I no longer had my 'best friend'—alcohol. And I was mourning its absence." At first this felt unnerving, even dangerous, and the fleeting urge to walk into a bar hit him like a quick punch in the gut. But he realized he didn't, after all, want to go back to being the drunk he'd been—he just wanted release. And slowly he began to feel a little release. Having allowed himself to have a full emotion, sober, was teaching him he could survive his own feelings and get the release he was after. It wasn't going to kill him.

The grief began to lift, and Brian felt the need to connect with his sponsor about it. He walked to the nearest pay phone, dialed the number, and got his sponsor's answering machine. This had always triggered his anger before, but now, for some reason, it was comforting enough just to make contact with his sponsor's voice on the tape. He then returned to work, apologized to his boss, and called up the client he'd yelled at to try to make amends. He felt, for this moment, cleansed. "It was like a storm had passed through. I'd withstood its passing and now enjoyed the clean, fresh feeling of its aftermath. I'd *survived a feeling*." What he had also done was face, for a moment, the fear that underlay it.

The primal fear that seems to underpin all our negative emotions can be paralyzing. We are so conditioned to respond to it by clenching or withdrawing or lashing out in anger, the most powerful reflexes a compulsive person knows. The process of doing a Fourth Step—the Step that suggests we do a "searching and fearless moral inventory" of ourselves—seems to provide the only means of facing that primal fear and the ways we've allowed it to paralyze us. What amazes people who engage in this inventory taking is that they often experience what Brian did after his storm: a cleansing. There's something about letting light in on fear that can automatically dissipate it, and a kind of spontaneous serenity can replace it.

I've learned from so many recovering compulsive people a simple, healing truth: allowing myself to undergo the full, start-to-finish breadth of a feeling almost always gets me to the "other side"—cleansed, refreshed, and generally better off. It's what we touched on earlier in this book: allowing yourself to fully experience your cravings (which are, after all, feelings) rather than jump in reflexively to act out on them, teaches you something about what you are really searching for, which always seems to be something more than a drink, a sexual encounter, or a snort of coke. That's what the experience of inventory taking can teach too. By allowing yourself to exist in what you feared would be the intolerable pain of certain emotions, you find that not only can you tolerate them but you actually can *thrive* in the learning experience they afford.

The very words "searching" and "fearless," which are the adjectives used to describe "inventory" in the Fourth Step, soon seem less moralistically intimidating; they become challenging, inviting, and adventurous. That's the sense of discovery you can feel by allowing yourself to "be with" your feelings. You're not out to gut yourself or demolish everything you find when you take stock of things. You're simply out to see what's there. The act of *seeing* can be healing all by itself. It also can start you on an incredible journey of self-discovery: you'll begin to see a pattern in what causes you shame, what you're afraid of, what you "hate." Not that this pattern necessarily reveals itself quickly. (I still don't know why I've got my chewing fixation; I only know I don't have to act like a lunatic when it bothers me!) But slowly, something deeper will begin to emerge, and the underlying motives for your resentments, fears, and hates will turn out to be something for which you feel compassion—even forgiveness. That's when the process of healing really takes hold.

I'm saying all this not only from my own experience but also from everyone who has told me about his own experience in inventory taking. It's not that everyone automatically "sees the light," because sometimes there are no immediate, dramatic benefits. But eventually the work of looking at ourselves this way pays off. Witness Brian, again, fresh from his

Fourth and Fifth Steps. (The Fifth Step is where you share what you've found "with God and another human being"— it's the essential act of giving away what you've found so you can be free, cleansed of it.) "I think the most incredible thing I discovered from my Fourth Step was how much of my motive was self-protective. Almost everything I'd done that I was ashamed of—lying, cheating, stealing—began to fall into a clear pattern. I was reacting in every case to some terrible fear. Basically, the fear of rejection and the fear of deprivation. I got the image of myself as a cornered animal. I'd obviously once felt that the only alternative was to lash out, go for the jugular. I was deeply convinced it was the only way to save myself—by destroying anyone or anything in my path."

Discovering this didn't, Brian says, absolve him of responsibility for the damage he had caused, but it did make him feel an amazing forgiveness. "I could accept myself as the monster that fear made me act like. But since I'd never given myself the chance to see what was making that monster the way he was, I was trapped. The only way I could deal with fear was to try desperately to repress it or, when that didn't work, act out on it. It's no wonder I was such a volcano!"

MENTAL WEATHER

My recovering friends have helped me discover an interesting perspective on feelings: they are a kind of mental weather. In Brian's words, he discovered that he could survive his feeling of grief: "It was like a storm had passed through. I'd withstood its passing and now enjoyed the clean, fresh feeling of its aftermath." What seems inescapable is that we cannot stop our feelings, fantasies, cravings, hates, fears, resentments, from welling up on us. They are as inevitable as wind and rain and sun. But we can learn to wait out the storms. We can learn that they will pass. It is enormously common for compulsive people to think that the way they are now is the way they'll always be. But if you look no further than your own experience, no further, usually, than this morning compared with this afternoon, you'll see you've been telling yourself a lie. You've already swept into a different position; things are already different.

"I try to think of my emotions like signposts," one compulsive friend of mine says. "What are they telling me? What needs looking at? I try not to be too convinced by whatever feeling is occurring at the moment. I try to keep from acting immediately on it. Acting on it impulsively is what always got me in trouble before." Another friend of mine puts it more strongly: "I wait for the first ten thousand feelings to pass. *Then* I decide what to do."

This may sound wonderfully levelheaded, but, of course, the heat of a strong emotion can make it very hard to keep from the old reflexive reactions. We all, God knows, make mistakes—emotional "slips." The reassuring watchwords in all Twelve Step programs are "Progress Not Perfection." But it does seem to be possible, over time, to develop the more buoyant perspective that we can survive the rough weather of our feelings. We have so much evidence already from the men in this book that it's possible. Bruno's marvelous discovery that he can listen—that he can withhold himself, calm down enough to experience the world without attempting to impose himself on it so it won't "go away"— is all part of the process of learning he can survive his feelings. Bruno, Mark, Jeremy, Rick, Brian, Peter, Grant, Matthew—all of these men give evidence that it's possible to *respond rather than react* to their feelings.

By their accounts, it's also a slow process to develop the kind of vigilance you need to withstand the onslaught of your own feelings without acting out. Brian, confronting his rage even in sobriety, learned this especially clearly: "It used to annoy me when someone in the program wished me a 'slow recovery.' Slow? I wanted it *now*—I wanted whatever the ultimate price was supposed to be, now. Then I realized that that was compulsive thinking. There is no ultimate prize. Life is a steady, unceasing, unpredictable stream. The trick is to learn to flow with it, and not pretend it's not happening or rage against my inability to change it. Now I'm grateful for the idea of slow recovery. It gives me the sense that I've got time. I don't have to figure all this out by next Tuesday. What a relief!"

Someone in a meeting I went to recently described the joy he was beginning to find in walking to work. He said that for most of his adult life, even in sobriety, he had sped as quickly as he could from home to office, impatient with any delay, grumbling at any red lights, at "stupid, slow people" in front of him, at irresponsible cab drivers who made right turns from the left lane, at the inept slow service he always seemed to get at the coffee shop where he picked up his take-out breakfast. He started to realize that he was habitually in a high state of stress. Then something snapped. He began looking around him. "The world was proceeding at its own leisurely pace, oblivious of my impatient storms and grumblings. Suddenly I saw it differently. Now the world seems to be *inviting* me to join it. I've been slowing down, enjoying the walk to work and feeling my body move, feeling the wind in my face, curious about other people on the street. It's like there was all this *abundance* I'd never noticed before. It was as if I'd been absent for most of my life."

"Showing up" for your life—allowing yourself to enjoy more of it and learning to tolerate what you can't enjoy—does take courage. You're obviously going to resist the decision not to run away when you've spent your life convinced that running away was the only alternative. But you've got so much help and support on tap; we've already seen that we don't have to walk unaccompanied through the door of recovery. Neither do we have to face our feelings alone. The help available is unbelievably abundant. Really facing the "truth" can't, in fact, happen in isolation—because the "truth" is that we're not isolated!

Emotions won't stop buffeting us. That's part of the "truth" too. The bottom line, says one old-timer I know in AA, is simply this: "There are good days and there are bad days." If I had told you this bit of wisdom at the beginning of this book, you might have slammed it shut. Now, perhaps, its simplicity seems a little less simplistic. You can survive both good days and bad days without resorting to acting out. And, if you're lucky, you may even thrive in the experience of surviving them. As Brian says, "I'm learning that the world is always an abundant place, even when it pisses me off."

Chapter Seven

Body Esteem: Getting Physical in Recovery

The dilemma of dealing with feelings in sobriety is one shared by every compulsive person, gay or straight, and apprehending our physical selves is a shared dilemma too. Physical sobriety is usually as much of a revelation as emotional sobriety. In some cases, "shock" is the better word. The abrupt, new sense of yourself without hangovers, without the relentless fatigue acting out caused you, without the barrage of bodily insults acting out entailed, can be astonishing. But it seems astonishing in a very interesting way to gay men.

An organic part of our growing self-esteem in sobriety seems to come from accepting that we *exist* physically. This is a radical notion to most gay male compulsives. We may have been able to accept ourselves fleetingly as sexual meat or as a fit body flashing in a store window or as a disembodied head we shaved by rote but were too afraid to really look at. (Remember Grant as he changed from a black T-shirt to a loose black sweater? He wouldn't look in the mirror so he wouldn't have to see if he looked "fat" without a shirt on.) But the notion of taking physical care of ourselves is often a foreign one. Real triumphs for us in sobriety often consist of joining a gym, taking out health insurance, seeing a doctor or dentist. We stumble into a whole new physical sense of ourselves, which seems to be an exact barometer of our self-love. Caring about our health instead of just our haircuts becomes a milestone. But our progress here can be slow and baffling. After years of either denying our physicality or associating it solely with sex, making sense of our bodies in sobriety can be a rough trip.

It's hard to link the words "physical" and "gay men" without jumping right into "sex." Compulsiveness defines the very notion of "gay men"—it's certainly the definition we've been brought up to believe about ourselves—in a way that it doesn't seem to define any other single group. Think: Men, women, children. (Czechs! Samoans!) Numerous images may arise, but does compulsive behavior have anything to do with them? Now think: Gay men. *Whoa*—here we go down the slide! What do we see in the *whoosh?* What do we feel, taste, smell? Skin—lots of skin. Sweat, Tuscany, and poppers. The feeling of Fire Island sand on your bare butt as you sunbathe (read "cruise") naked in the dunes. Bitchy laughter and ice cubes against glass, an endless slew of brunch and cocktails. Subway men's rooms, the smell of disinfectant mingling with urine. The echo of heavy breathing in tiled rooms. The heady scent of men at the gym, and the choking steam of a sauna while you try to make out who's "available" in the mist. The drone of disco in a dark bar, pushed up against crowds of men, each of whom is acting as if nobody else were there. These "popular" images of the gay male are ones with which we've saturated ourselves for decades, and they are full of the imagery of compulsion. The bottom line is gay-male-as-physical-body. We are how we look. We are how we're hung. We are nothing but what we desperately poke, prod, pump up, or corset our *meat* into being.

To some degree, we can identify with the image women have had thrust on them. Seeing ourselves in abject terms of physical attractiveness, we—like many women—are extraordinarily self-conscious about our looks. But we're also *men*, and what that generally means in western culture is that we've been brought up to be sexual predators. While the strong subliminal message women have had to swallow is passivity, we—even those of us who spent our boyhoods feeling decidedly different from the conventional male— were programmed in a range of ways to "aggress." What this means in the average gay bar is that you've got a lot of predators and no prey. For one predator to succumb to another, the one who wins had better be damned good. He'd better be the best exemplar of maleness we can get. And so had we, if we ever hope to be gotten ourselves.

The pressure we put on ourselves is crushing. From listening to hundreds of gay compulsive men across the country, it's clear to me that the toll of squeezing ourselves into the prevailing gay image has been terrible. It's not that we haven't squeezed a fair amount of "pleasure" out of the attempt. As we've seen throughout this book, the quick fixes to which we've compulsively turned have some very definable—and, at least for a while, reliable—pleasures. But defining "gay" solely in terms of these pleasures has squeezed the humanity out of us, not to mention having contributed mightily to the urge to act out compulsively.

It seems that for a gay man to be sober, he has to face some painful realizations about who he is physically—realizations, rather, that may *begin* as painful but can eventually lead us to an unprecedented serenity about who we are physically. Most of us have stories about feeling inadequate in sports or gym class as kids, but that's just the tip of the iceberg. Let's allow a man named Joe to take us further and give us a sense of what it requires to learn to feel comfortable in our bodies as well as our minds. It's a highly sensitive area for gay men (if you'll forgive the pun), and one that pleads for our attention. What we think of ourselves physically feeds directly into our compulsions, as you'll soon see.

PHYS ED: HORROR EROTICIZED

"Why do gay boys hate gym class so much?" Joe asks. "I hate to make generalizations about us, but I don't think I've ever met a gay man who didn't suffer excruciating humiliation in phys ed. Always being the last to be picked for a team. Suffering taunts like 'you throw like a girl.' Jeered at whenever we picked up a bat, mitt, or football." Today, Joe looks as if he'd have had no trouble in gym. He works out regularly and exudes good health. But he says he was no different from any other gay boy he's since heard about. "I dreaded gym class in junior high. I dreaded having to take my clothes off in front of other boys—much as I craved a peek at them. But I felt, automatically, inadequate in their eyes. And when I got out onto the football field or the basketball court or the track, I felt like a prisoner in jail, as if I were incarcerated for some unnameable sin whose punishment was to be made a fool of." Joe says, "It wasn't that I was uncoordinated, especially. It was just"—he pauses, trying to come up with an explanation of gym-phobia that all too often stumps the rest of us too—"I'd always felt so apart from the other boys. I'd always felt different. I didn't give a damn about baseball. Maybe that just sapped my self-confidence so much that I felt defeated before I started. Ball games were for *normal* kids, not me."

Whatever it was, Joe says he still cringes from the memory of being taunted as a kid, being called a sissy and a faggot long before he or any of his tormentors really knew what a faggot was. All Joe knew is that it was something unspeakable and that he was whatever loathsome thing it meant. Joe did everything he could to get out of gym class—scheduling his clarinet lessons during gym period, playing sick—whatever he could think of. But he still had to put up with it most of the time, and his feelings of inadequacy deepened. What feeling inadequate also seemed to do, however, was fuel the attractiveness of boys who could play sports. He developed strong crushes on some of the jocks who'd abused him most: basketball and wrestling and football stars whom he couldn't help fantasizing about when he masturbated. It seemed the more Joe learned to hate himself for being physically inadequate, the more he craved the guys who'd told him he was.

Joe was especially turned on by the school's basketball team. "Those guys were usually the most physically mature—they were the tallest—and I drove myself mad with fantasies of all those long, lean bodies." When Joe's father noticed his son's interest in watching basketball on television, he was thrilled. "It was the first time he'd seen me interested in anything 'normal,' " Joe said. "But I couldn't stand my father's corny, buddy-buddy remarks about the game. He thought I was interested in the *sport*. He didn't know I was getting a hard-on over the *players*." Because Joe felt guilty about the sexual nature of his interest in all those basketball players, he started to watch games in secret, changing the channel whenever his father walked into the room. He would collect clippings from the sports pages or spreads from *Sports Illustrated* for his personal pornography pile. "I'd fixate on how this one guy's muscular arm looked stretched up toward the basket, a curl of hair from his chest over the top of his shirt, the sweat on his brow—that peculiar look of *sexual* intensity athletes get when they concentrate hard—the long, huge muscles of his legs, the stretch of satin across his ass. . . ." Joe has to check himself. The images are still very powerful and dangerous. It all pulls Joe back to his compulsion.

Joe began to lose himself in his "pornography" collection. He would spend hours beating off to his favorite pictures. Closing the door to his room, he would spread all of the hottest ones across the bed and tack others up on the wall until his whole room looked like a shrine to straining, sweating basketball players. But "straight" sports reportage wasn't quite satisfying enough, especially as he began to grow bored with the same old pictures. Photos would only capture "hot" poses by chance. Joe wanted more. So he started writing his own sports/porn stories, and then doing drawings.

"I'd always been talented in art. Now I started to use that talent to turn myself on. I began doing locker-room scenarios; when they gave me a hard-on and made me want to beat off, I knew I'd succeeded." Drawing and writing his own pornography became his primary pastime. It began to crowd out everything else in his life. Every moment he could spend away from "real life" he devoted to his fantasies. They consumed his time, his mind, his energy.

By the time Joe was in his twenties, he had developed a thriving but guilt-inducing correspondence with other guys he had attracted through ads in gay papers and magazines, ads that proclaimed his obsession with "locker-room action— especially b-ball players." He rarely met any of the men who wrote back; acting out on their shared fantasies was almost always disappointing. The few times he did, it was almost always a bust. The guys never were as attractive as he had hoped, and there was always a guilty, furtive, depressing quality to sharing sex and pornography in the flesh. It diminished the fantasy he could embellish in the privacy of his own imagination. It drained him, making him feel small and worthless, even smaller and more worthless than he was already on the way to feeling by keeping to himself. So his drawings became the focus—and masturbation his obsessive outlet.

His correspondents began offering him money to do more drawings to order. Joe would spend lunch hours at his desk at work when everyone else had gone, drawing in a fevered pitch, massaging his crotch after each stroke of the pencil, totally consumed by the fantasies he drew. Then he would photocopy them, experimenting with light and dark on the copy machine until he got just the "hot" chiaroscuro he was after. "Copying those drawings was almost the best part," Joe says. "They always looked darker and better than the originals, as if the machine were making them for me. The funny thing was, I did some of my best drawings then. I was so filled with excitement that I guess it communicated itself. But it was becoming too much. Pornography had taken over my life."

Joe's drawings began to backfire in some excruciatingly embarrassing ways. He accidentally left the original of an extremely explicit locker-room sex scene in the copy machine. His boss, a straitlaced woman of about sixty, discovered it. "She looked down at it in horror," Joe says. "I guess I should be able to laugh about it now—but my heart stopped. Worse, she'd suspected I did it. She glanced quickly at me with wide eyes, then crumpled the page up as if it were a piece of toilet paper. Not a word was said, but I felt like killing myself." More drawings accidentally got clipped to correspondence that then got filed. My boss called me in and said in even, slow tones that she wasn't paying me to perform my perversions in her office and she would no longer be needing my services. It was like my worst nightmare come true. Somehow that lady became my mother, every teacher I'd ever had, every authority figure I'd ever quaked in front of. I felt like garbage."

Joe went into therapy and into a Twelve Step sexual addiction program at the suggestion of his therapist. Discovering the beginnings of relief from his addiction in ways we've already chronicled, he began by surrendering to his powerlessness over pornography. The first surrender has led to others. Much as we've seen serial revelations happen in the lives of other men we've met in this book, Joe began, on deeper and deeper levels, to accept the self-hate that was really fueling his compulsion. It went back to his earliest fantasies in elementary school gym. Somehow he had accepted the definition of himself as physically inept; somehow that also automatically meant sexualizing other boys who were good at what he was so awful at. "I began to have a little compassion for myself. Slowly it seemed very clear that I was projecting onto these other boys my own desperate desire to be adequate, eroticizing them in the process, clinging to my fantasies because my craving to be 'adequate' was so strong." But that wasn't the only feeling that's come up. "I also feel outraged, sometimes," Joe says. "How dare anybody measure a boy's or a man's worth by whether or not he can throw a ball! It suddenly seems monstrously unfair that I've been cringing all these years under that judgment."

On this one point—rage at how we were treated because we couldn't throw a ball—gay men seem to rally most passionately. The anger and the frustration and the *shame* we all felt! From the vantage point of adulthood, it can seem silly. But the pain of feeling "less than" was so severe that few of us don't wince at it even now.

Joe realized gradually, in therapy and by working the Twelve Steps, that he had to face this shame if he were ever to get over it and free himself from his pornography compulsion—a compulsion that he could now, rationally, see was provoked by shame. He never thought he would ever have the nerve to join a gym. Somehow the gay men he knew who did work out were as foreign to him as any straight man voluntarily playing softball for fun. They all seemed to be a species different from him. But one day, lured by a special discount rate offered by a "straight" gym, Joe actually walked in and allowed himself to be shown the premises. He was glad it wasn't a gay gym both because it would have been too much of a temptation to fantasize about all the men and because he was afraid he would make such a fool of himself in front of gay "hunks." ("I envisioned straining with ten-pound weights while Mr. Porn Star next to me lifted the equivalent of a Mack truck.") This gym, he felt, was tailor-made: it had old people and women and out-of-shape businessmen—no one he'd be threatened by. "I felt like a closet gymgoer," Joe laughs. "No gay man I know would have been caught dead at this place."

On the first day, Joe was brought through the Nautilus routines and was amazed at how doable they were. Already his confidence had increased. Then he was taught how to work out with free weights, which had always seemed to him so impossibly macho, but which now seemed like perfectly normal exercise. Every new set he did filled him with unaccustomed pride: he—little Joe, the wimp!—was doing what *they* did. It's not that it was so easy. In fact, it was the strain of working out that helped Joe the most. His locker-room fantasies *were* fantasies because he'd never had any experience of "real" athletes and exercise. Now that he was gaining that experience, working out seemed a little less glamorous, more de-sexualized. He added aerobics to his regiment—starting, for the first time in his life, to run. ("I never thought I'd turn into one of those yuppie joggers," Joe says, "but now I can't stay off the track.") He discovered something completely unexpected. Not only did he like to run but it helped him to meditate, to calm down, to, again, de-sexualize rather than fuel his fantasies.

All of this gym experience happened in tandem with therapy and Twelve Step meetings. Joe's adjustment to it is his own. Not everyone who has compulsive fantasies about jocks and locker rooms loses them by turning into a jock himself. But Joe's experience is still worth remarking on because it shows that, sometimes, allowing yourself to gain competence in a "forbidden" area can drain it of its forbidden allure. Increased self-esteem seems to be a by-product. "I no longer feel I'm inept, physically," Joe says. "I even wonder why I ever did feel that way, sometimes. I can remember how bad I felt as a kid, but somehow turning things around now is taking care of the hurt kid I was. Facing my shame by proving to myself that I could be 'physical' has had any number of benefits. Not the least of them is that I'm not so riveted anymore by my old fantasies. I've let some light onto them, and suddenly they're not so potent anymore."

Joe's experience is Joe's; it may not be yours. I have to say it wasn't, for a long time, mine. Like Joe, I had a similar awakening by joining a gym—a straight gym too—and it *was* wonderful discovering I could actually figure out what to do with all those complicated machines. But I had a hard time adjusting to paying this new kind of attention to myself. It might help you to hear about the gym's effect on me, if only to add counterpoint to Joe's experience.

My physical awareness of myself has had rocky ups and downs, unpredictable fits and starts. Like so many other recovering alcoholics, I marveled in the early days of my sobriety that I suddenly could sleep better and digest food better. Suddenly I wasn't throwing up anymore, suddenly my chronic diarrhea disappeared, and my incipient diverticulosis cleared up. I even lost weight. At 5-10, I'd ballooned up to about two hundered pounds of bloat; now that I wasn't deluged with alcohol's empty calories, a good thirty or so pounds of that dropped off. The idea of joining a gym came to me as a sort of domino effect: now that I was feeling so much better physically, I felt able to accept myself a little better—which meant I began wanting to take care of myself. But joining the gym, revelatory as it was, triggered some difficulties. One of them was a simple one: I quickly realized that caloric expenditure on Nautilus machines is just about nil. I realized this by discovering I was putting on weight despite working out, slowly inching back up to 190 pounds. Then I made a decision to go on a crash diet. I may have acquired some alcoholic sobriety, but I hadn't a clue about what to do about food and its effect on my body—except, for this period, to cut it down to nearly zero. Like our friend Grant, I went down to about 800 calories a day and lost 40 pounds in about four months— from 186 pounds to 145. It is *not* a diet I would recommend.

I wouldn't recommend it not only because of its nutritional dangers but also because it fed a sense of *myself* that was dangerous. I nearly lost myself in the crazed attempt to get thin. It was a traumatic—and (I guess) interesting—enough experience to make me want to write about it. And so I did, in a piece published by *The New York Native* entitled "Stripping Down to the Id," which I'm offering here again. It seemed to touch a nerve in a lot of people. Also, it conveys the "heat" I was feeling then better than I could convey it, in different words, today. Today, thank God, I've found a bit more serenity about my physical self. But *then,* as I wrote, "my life has turned into a story Kafka ought to have written. . . ."

STRIPPING DOWN TO THE ID

Some wild creature has been let loose in me and is running the show; the console's lit up and buzzing, and the mission is clear: *You cannot be too skinny.* I am riveted by such things as "Club Kids" on the cover of *New York* magazine, all painted faces and frail thin limbs. I gawk at East Villagers, walking black pencils, thin sharp spikes of hair and swatches of bare skin zapping out from scrawny backs, asses and thighs. I am riveted because I'm fifteen years older than most of them and the crazy creature running the console inside me is squeezing me down to their size, drip by drip. I have calculated myself down to smallness. I have lost nearly 25 percent of myself.

I pass Goldbar (chic on its glass door as GOLD BAR) on East Ninth Street just west of First Avenue. When I was heavy, I used to think of it as the 28-Inch Waist Club, and thus forever closed to me. Now that my own waist has whittled down to that size, I still feel like an outsider. I am still not the insouciant, uncaring kind of "thin" that the black-T-shirted bugle boys within seem to be. They are thin because they're young. I am thin because I'm crazy. The need to look at this and be honest about it fights the blind compulsion to simply get thinner.

Here's where my compulsion lives, the fantasy it paints,

the 28-Inch Waist Club my wild creature searches out: a gray, barren, after-hours GOLD BAR, glass-windowed so that everyone inside is visible. But the night outside is Edward Hopper empty, not a soul on the sidewalk. The twenty-four boys inside are obliviously long limbed, sleek. Lithe, libidinous. Sex is the air they breathe. They are Aldous Huxley's *Brave New World*—thoughtless perfection, the slightest unsightliness banished from their bodies, not a possibility. Thin bodies in a mist of self-absorption, taut male Hepburns (Kate and Audrey) artfully draped for, and available only to, themselves. Inaccessible to the street out there, unavailable for comment. Long, ropy, muscular, light bad boys. Kids whose hormones have burst them into grown-up bodies. Wraparound muscle. Four A.M. eyes. A steady pulse of sex in the blood, as quiet and confident as cats.

This is the fantasy my creature at the console plays for me. It is why I walk into the Young Men's sections of stores and buy cotton pants with 28-inch waists.

I am stripping down to the Id.

It's absolutely exhausting. I can tell it's exhausting not only because the constant, rapid caloric computations in my head—the sharp-edged, endlessly detailed comparisons between his ass and his ass and his ass and my ass—make me feel tired. It is also that, when I look in the mirror, I see my skull shrinking from my hair, of which there suddenly seems too much. Veins I've never seen before stand out in my neck. Bags appear under my eyes.

Why do I not look twenty-two?

Perhaps because I was born in 1951.

Daily caloric deprivations squeeze the juice out of me along with the fat. Can I afford to lose all this? My head blares like a disco: *Yes you can. Get thin. Get thinner.*

I try health—or at least the gym. The console screams red at the thought.

Now that there's less fat on me, my muscles show. I transfix myself in the mirror, watching my biceps contract and lengthen, pop up and rope out. This is me I'm looking at, I need to keep telling myself. The self-congratulation is thick, a downpour of narcissism. I can hardly stand myself in the mirror. I give myself a hard-on.

Does this happen to other gay men? To straight men? Do other men beat off at the thought of themselves? I'm down a long road now, where Kafka meets John Rechy, and William Burroughs licks his chops. MeMeMeMe on the rack, slick with sweat and braided as a rope. Here I am, for their and my own delectation. I cannot get enough.

I cannot get enough because the self-congratulation won't stay congratulatory. Unless I vigilantly keep pumping up the fantasy, it decomposes into self-hate. The flip side of delectation is disgust. Desperate attempts at self-love are desperate because they're up against self-loathing. I need to keep the fire of fantasy going because I dread the thought of facing myself without its furious light and heat. Fantasy is my fuel. It replaces calories, keeps my hope in motion, tells me I'll reap untold rewards if only I keep at it.

Which is, of course, the problem. Now that I'm "thin," my psyche is revved up for an apocalypse, but because those rewards don't come, or because those that do come—I can wear clothes I've never worn before and I look reasonably good in a bathing suit—haven't catapulted me into an inexorable state of bliss, my psyche goads me to the only conclusion compulsion will allow: I'm obviously not thin enough.

Serenity does not this way lie. Serenity, in fact, isn't a

possibility as long as I keep fueling myself with fantasy instead of food.

What is this on button I've found and why can't I seem to find the off switch? Here I am what Wallis Simpson said you can't be too much of, and I'm berserk when I'm not miserable. I've accomplished a goddam American dream, haven't I? Aren't you insanely jealous? Don't you think I'm a nutcase for hating my 28-inch waist when I don't slaver over it? Why is there no joy in Mudville tonight?

When I calm my *angst*-ridden self down enough to take a peek at what's really bothering me, when I look at what perhaps few average Americans would call a "problem" about my dwindling physical self ("He's complaining about *what*?"), when I try to clear away the heat of the fantasy and the internal roar of the creature at the console's message ("thin, thinner, *thinner*"), I see two problems which don't sweep away when the steam does. They are incredibly simple. They are even what may turn my particular neurosis into something universal—nay, commonplace:

I want to be loved.

I don't want to grow old.

Wonder diets don't tell you much about that. Suddenly, the kids at the 28-Inch Waist Club look a little different.

They look hungry.

The "hunger" I wrote about then is still poignant to me now, almost three years later. Sometimes it's more than poignant—I do still sometimes crave *attention* the way I found myself craving it back then. I said before that this piece seemed to hit a nerve: it was interesting to me to get responses not only from other gay men but also from heterosexual men and women friends of mine who identified strongly with the self-mistrust that underlies desperate attempts to get "thin"—desperate attempts to get "beautiful." We are, all of us, so needy for love—and the more compulsive we are, the more urgent our need seems to be for absolute, nth-degree love—something that will, once and for all, *take care of us,* abolish pain and fear forever, and make us feel safe and wanted and complete. The creatures at our console play one blaring tune at us, night and day: "Do whatever it takes to get safe!" And so we scramble for whatever we convince ourselves that has to be. If we stumble onto something as potent as the prospect of being thought physically "beautiful," we're often immediately lost in fantasy and greed because it seems the perfect ticket to acceptance, the perfect ticket to being loved in that imagined nth-degree way.

I take a long deep breath at the memory of the hell I pushed myself through back then, the hell that sometimes beckons to me now in the guise of an alluring paradise. But now that I'm a little better at getting down to the motives I was only able to uncover with great difficulty back then, now that I can see and accept my need for love, my fear of mortality, I don't get as hoodwinked by that hell's promises. Once I simply *let go* of my fear—"turn over" my life to the care of "God *as I understand him*" (to paraphrase the Third Step)—I find an abundant source of serenity. I'm better, less besieged. And the creature at my console takes a nap.

The self-obsession we've seen in "Stripping Down to the Id" almost always hides some variant of self-hate. I know so many extraordinarily handsome right-off-the-pages-of-*GQ*-or-*Mandate* gay compulsive men who have fought the most terrible self-views—who desperately poke, prod, pump up, and corset the *meat* of themselves because it's the only way they can imagine feeling even remotely "adequate." As one of these men puts it, "I spent my whole life thinking that if I could be perfect, I'd at least be *marginally* acceptable." The famous sullen attitude pose—sneer turned to stance—that gay men purport to hate about other gay men soon seems the purest projection. Because we've so deeply rejected ourselves, we communicate "rejection" almost by reflex. Straining to turn how we look into a ticket to acceptance provides very precarious pleasure and security.

This is a more than interesting observation to compulsive gay men: anxiety about who we are externally so often has led us to act out, either to blot out our feelings of inadequacy or to celebrate the triumph of convincing the world out there that we are, after all, "hot." I don't know any gay man who isn't touched by this tyranny; I don't know any gay compulsive man who isn't gravely endangered by it.

Luckily, when we put the focus on love and service, when we put the focus on striving to see similarities among us rather than who is closer to a "10" than a "3"—when we focus on the kind of internal stock-taking that Twelve Step programs suggest we try—in short, when we pour energy into our recovery, a lot of the anxiety we have about our bodies begins to lift. As we've seen so often before, this lifting is a kind of dividend; it's not something that happens because we've attacked it head-on in some strained act of willpower. Joe turned to the gym as a process of learning to like himself better, and liking himself better meant he spontaneously wanted to take care of himself better.

Some Ph.D. candidate could do a fascinating and lengthy treatise on addicts and their teeth. I never cease to wonder at this correlation. It seems that teeth, apart from whatever mysterious sexual symbolism they may have had to Freud, indicate our feeling of self-worth to an almost unbelievable degree. I've been to so many Twelve Step meetings of every stripe where the triumph of the day was that someone had actually—for the first time in five, eight, ten, fifteen years— gone to the dentist. This almost never fails to elicit groans of empathy, spontaneous applause, and a sea of waving hands ("Wait 'til you hear about my root canal!"). I won't venture too much dime-store psychology, at least not past the general observation that opening your mouth and allowing an Authority Figure (the ubiquitously feared Dentist) to peer in is making yourself vulnerable to what you're sure will be the Authority Figure's scathing denunciations. ("How could you do this to yourself?") But you're also opening yourself up to intimacy; in a very obvious way, you're letting someone *in!* Letting a dentist into your mouth, for some of us, is a little like Dorian Gray letting someone up into the attic to check on the progress of that painting. It's humbling. It's honest. It's an implicit plea for understanding—and help.

In the same way, turning to doctors marks triumph for so many of us. It's almost insulting to remind anyone reading this book that AIDS is the first thing we think of when we get a sore throat or find a pimple. For compulsive gay men—so used to denying our own reality—facing up to physical discomfort and taking appropriate measures to deal with it *isn't,* to put it mildly, what we normally do. I am so moved when I see an addict, no matter what his addiction, make the decision to seek medical help.

A friend of mine who'd had a major phobia about hospitals, along with a lifelong belief that he didn't "deserve" good treatment by anyone, least of all himself, made the decision a year ago to have some varicose veins removed. He astonished himself: to do something so purely cosmetic (and in a hospital) was once *far* beyond the realm of possibility for him. I visited him in his hospital room the night before his operation. He was like a little boy—his forty-five years melted down to about twelve. He looked up at me expectantly and said, "Wanna see what they're taking out?" Then, again like an eager boy, he proudly lifted the sheet to show me his leg, as if to get my approval of the *need* for the operation. When I saw him after it was over, he had gained something indefinable, a glow of accomplishment, a strong light in his eyes that spoke volumes about his increased self-esteem. This was a man who, not two years before, would have retreated to a flophouse hotel room to suck on a quart of vodka before he'd used a toothbrush, and here he was, now, taking care of himself in undreamed-of ways.

The ways we can learn to take care of ourselves physically usually *are* undreamed of. The catch seems to be that the better we look as the result of taking care of ourselves in sobriety, the more we can be tempted to see ourselves in the old purely vain and self obsessed physical ways—witness, again, my painful narcissism in the gym. But recovery can always continue. "You can start your day over any time," one wise friend counsels me. Sharing with others how you feel is always a recourse. So is working the Steps. So is reminding yourself of something that seems to be crucial: the physical improvement and growing self-esteem you're feeling are the result of *not* acting out. They are a dividend, and, like any dividend, something to be grateful for because it could so easily be taken away. Gratitude almost always pushes away self-centeredness. When we are grateful, we are outward-directed. We're automatically "open" and don't feel we're the source of our own good fortune as much as we feel it's a *gift.* There's humility in feeling grateful, an openness that softens us and makes us receptive. I was so unnerved at the first Twelve Step meetings I went to because there were so many people in the rooms who looked transcendently beautiful in ways I'd never seen in a bar, a disco, or the baths. They had allowed sobriety to soften them, open them, make them receptive—and the light they now allowed to shine through was extraordinary. No Nautilus machine can jam that light into you. You can't put it on with a brush.

Our negative self-views, and especially the negative views we have of our physical selves, are so deeply rooted that this softening process, the process by which we learn to love ourselves and then actually take *care* of ourselves, is usually a very slow one. The shame we have about what we've done to and with our bodies, the huge inadequacies most of us have been taught to feel about ourselves physically—none of this drops away overnight. Not that there isn't a kind of magic that allows them eventually to drop away in Twelve Step recovery. But if it's magic, it comes from a completely reliable and simple source. There's no hocus-pocus about it. It's the magic that comes from self-acceptance, self-love. Gratitude and humility, one helpful friend of mine often says, are the "wonder drugs" that can allow that magic to blossom and nurture you. They are two of Twelve Step programs' most powerful tools.

Add these to love and service and you've got quite a tool kit. Love, service, gratitude, and humility: no matter what your addiction, no matter what bump in the rug you're prone to trip over, this quartet can work wonders. It can even help you in what may seem a more mine-laden stretch of territory than your own body or how you feel about yourself physically. It can even help when you face the prospect of sharing your body—and self—with *another* man.

You may think "sober love" is an oxymoron, but friends of mine show me that's not true. What they've discovered (and can allow us to discover) about love between two men comes next.

Chapter Eight

The Shock of Loving a Man

I had to ask myself if what seems to be a bias toward sex as a topic in this book is my own bias or if, as I'd rather think, it reflects an emphasis I've heard throughout the country from hundreds of gay compulsive men. I do know that even if it *is* an issue I'm drawn to for personal reasons, it's clear that I'm not the only one drawn to it. And it's clear, in the more "objective" data of the notes I've taken, that sexual and romantic compulsions are phenomena that afflict the vast majority of gay men who describe themselves as compulsive. Even if they don't go to programs like Sexaholics Anonymous (SA) or SLAA or SCA, when compulsive gay men speak about the role of sex and love in their lives they clearly are dealing with the same issues dealt with by members of those groups.

Perhaps we shouldn't be surprised. As suggested in the last chapter, the very notion of "gay man" is steeped in sex. That's what "gay" means to most of the world: what we do in bed. Because that's what allegedly sets us apart from everybody else on the planet, that's how everybody else on the planet feels compelled to define us: sexually.

Up until recently, it's a definition of "gay" most of us have been, if not content with, then at least unthinkingly resigned to applying to ourselves. Compulsive gay men are, however, at the cutting edge of some new definitions as they attempt to recover from their compulsivity. They are at the cutting edge not because they're especially more prescient than other people but because, in learning to save their lives, they've had to come up with broader definitions for "gay" than sexual ones. Gay men who define themselves as sexually or romantically compulsive, or "co-dependent," or addicted in any way to what prove to be unhealthy emotional relationships, are discovering that they *have* to see relationships between men differently because the old ways were destroying them. There is an urgency in redefining terms for us that goes far beyond the semantic.

Unearthing old assumptions about what's possible between two men and attempting to replace them with something better is, looked at in its totality, a giant job. But men who are recovering from compulsion in these areas seem to be discovering that it is possible, one fraction of an assumption at a time. Revelations soon become commonplace; we have so much to learn from one another. One of the most arresting of these revelations has, for me, come from staring the beast in the face—quite literally. Take the same look I recently did, and see what you think.

LOOKING INTO THE EYES OF A PORN STAR

There are, you will remember, two general archetypes of porn star. One is the sullen, indifferent, bored stud, ready to service or be serviced, but not about to get emotional about it. The other is the guy who cruises, achingly, whose eyes *beseech*. These archetypes are not only sexually arousing to gay men, they also subtly define our expectations—not only of what good porn is but of what love and sex *off* the screen are supposed to be. Or so it seems from what I'm told by other recovering sex and love addicts, and so it certainly seems from my own experience.

The urge to have sex, whichever archetype you fantasize yourself to be or want, is the urge to be *sated,* and for a sexual compulsive, this means having so much that it becomes too much. The only respite is exhaustion, not satisfaction. You feel a temporary sense of release and (sometimes or variously) peace, contentment like after a meal, nostalgic sadness, depression, numbness—until the huge urge to be filled takes over again. Most sexual compulsives will tell you this whole apparatus of an urge has little to do with being horny. Although, on the rare occasion you are aware of being *physically* horny because you've abstained from orgasm for a long enough time (if you're actively sexually compulsive, this will probably be very rare indeed), you leap into the fray with incredible gusto. Sex, at these times, seems relatively "normal" and thus (finally! you think to yourself) "justified." ("Don't want to get blue balls, do I?") You've got an excuse for acting out, very much like alcoholics use Christmas, birthdays, St. Patrick's Day, New Year's Day, and many other holidays to "justify" their drinking. Look out for the compulsive when he's got even a glimmer of self-justification! He is never more out of control; it's potent fuel, that feeling of being "justified."

But, justified or not, an hour after you've come, you want more—even if it's not more orgasmic release. You want the release, somehow, of contact. You want validation that you're "attractive." It's no secret why so many gay men seek sex with the urgency they do: with the history many of us had of being branded eggheads or aesthetes, the prospect of being apprehended as pure, dumb meat has an irresistible allure. It's as close as some of us can imagine to being loved "unconditionally"—not for our clever accomplishments but simply for the mute *flesh* we are.

Our desire might be for unconditional love, but, in most of the gay sexual world, we've quickly clamped conditions on the sexual selves we are or seek—it matters terribly how *attractive* we are as men. We have become as destructively, coldly competitive as any junior high gym-class team that used to turn us down. Now we turn one another down with the same ruthlessness—or pick one another with the same exploitative urge. Either we're useful ("hot") or useless (not "hot"). Love doesn't have much place in this game, at least not externally. It's ironic that gay men are, in most cases justifiably, praised for our sensitivity, for our ability to empathize and understand, but we can, in the service of compulsive sex, turn into the most heartless beasts, reverting to meat whenever we can, seeking to obliterate nuance and ambiguity and confusion and doubt and pain and humor. Nothing is more deadly than somebody giggling during sexual acting out; a cheerful conversation overheard in a sexual acting-out place is a real bummer and cause for great resentment because it's a painful reminder that we're *not* meat. It's a painful reintroduction of an "outside," fuller reality, which we're doing everything in our power to escape.

Sexual compulsion that *depends* on anonymous contact does so for exactly this reason: new meat means new distraction, and we'll never have to know the sensitive being it hides. Second encounters with the same man are almost always less exciting, more disappointing than first encounters. (Is it any wonder many sexual compulsives lose sexual interest in lovers? If you start losing interest during the second encounter with someone, what will you be like after the two hundred and second?) The only thing that might help you to sustain interest is if the game you play ensures that both of you *stay* meat—the ritualized top and bottom in s&m sex or the playing out of a vivid, clearly delineated fantasy whose purpose is to dehumanize, whose structure is confining enough to keep you reduced to your role, giving you the illusion that your "role" is all you need (if you can just fill it completely).

Someone (to put it bluntly) who gives great head becomes a sex machine, not a man with feelings and a personality who has sex out of choice and love or as an integrated part of his life. No wonder poppers are so popular. More than any other recreational drug, they give a temporary localized rush that allows you to glorify the mechanics of the sexual act—to block out all else except *body*. There seems to be an element, if not generally in male sexuality then certainly in most male sexual compulsives, that depends on tunnel vision, or focused concentration; you seek an atmosphere that allows you to focus on mechanics. Think of pornographic settings and real settings for acting out: wharves, gyms, garages, locker rooms. The metal and wood and rough get-down-to-it macho "structure" of these places makes them erotic not only because they're culturally defined as the nth degree of "male" but also because they obliterate "soft" emotions. And sexual compulsives of a certain variety want nothing soft. At least on the surface.

What we've described is the fantasy world of the first porn archetype: the sullen, indifferent stud. But looking into the eyes of the second archetype holds some different surprises.

There is a hidden *ache* for tender contact that does get expressed even in the hard contexts of gyms and piers and garages. In fact, it's remarkable how much tenderness gets expressed in tearooms and parks and porno movie houses. This is the sexual compulsive's most shameful secret: he wants to caress, to hold, to kiss, to nuzzle a warm neck, to express affection—even to hold hands. The hard-core compulsive may consign these secretive gestures to "foreplay" or "afterplay," but—again secretly—they often constitute the most important component of the whole "act." The barely acknowledged sense is, however, that these are dividends— subsidiary to the Main Event. We usually don't allow ourselves to accept these passing, furtive, tender gestures as "important" or "the point." The point, we tell ourselves, is mechanistic sex.

But, in fact, the most furtive aspect of compulsive anonymous sex often isn't the sex itself—it's the silent, blind, tender gesture. This is the soul reaching out. And the soul *will* reach out, no matter if you're in a men's room stall or an orgy room of a backroom bar. We know this, deeply—we *all* know this—but we hide it as if it were the most terrible, inadmissible secret of all.

In fact, that ache for tenderness is the *source* of recovery.

Let's look into our porn stars' eyes now. Let's focus on these men solely from the neck up, for a change. Is there not a kind of infinite, inchoate promise in this first encounter that has nothing to do with sex? Remember the *beginning* of almost any porn film. Remember what was going on in the *eyes*. Don't, for the moment, assume the inevitable—that they'll soon take off their clothes and have sex. Stay with their first looks, the beseeching of their eyes, and translate those looks for yourself. What's the real unspoken dialogue? Gaze into the eyes of an imaginary "hot" man. What do they say?

"You look like you'll do it."

Do what?

"Satisfy me."

What needs satisfying?

"*You* know what."

Why?

"Because I'm horny."

Why?

Because I need . . ."

What?

"Because I need contact, love, connection. Because my soul aches for release—relief. Relief from how alone I feel. From how terrified I am. I want to be loved. That's all. *Just love me.*"

The soul can triumph in the oddest places. If we can find it in the eyes of a stud in a porno movie, we can find it in ourselves. Having the courage to go past the first questions, to tolerate the deeper ones and the deeper feelings, means answering what's beneath "Let's have sex." Tolerating our craving so that we've got the real chance of meeting it—of alleviating the ache.

What I hope I've just done is help you into and *through* a craving—to come out the other side of it so that it's clear that the craving wasn't what it seemed, at first, to be. When I suggested that the source of recovery lay in our "ache for tenderness," I mean that it is by recognizing and paying attention to our deepest needs that we begin to get a real idea of what we want. As I discovered in "Stripping Down to the Id," my narcissistic gym-going and obsession about my weight were really about (once the "steam" of my compulsion cleared) my desperate desire for love—to *be* loved. It was by locating that desire in myself that I could begin to unmask my compulsion for the guise it really was.

None of this takes away from the surrender, taking inventory, love and service process of the Twelve Steps as the way to recover from compulsion. I'm simply passing on a perspective about compulsion I've been given in Twelve Step meetings: our cravings, as we've seen before so often in this book, can be our truest guides, if we'll only allow ourselves to tolerate them long enough to see what they're actually telling us; if we'll only, in other words, not act out.

God knows that when two "real" human beings get together, especially if one or both of those human beings is a compulsive gay man, seeing through cravings can seem all but impossible. We sometimes are attracted to one another's "dis-ease"—and what passes for conversation among us can be one disease talking to another. But sometimes even that can set the stage for a breakthrough. Witness the following story about Steven and how he had to rework his ideas of "love" and "gay men" (and a man named Michael) from the ground up.

REPAIRING THE BRUTALIZED HEART

Steven, like a number of men we've met in this book, is the survivor of an alcoholic family. In his case, both his mother and father were alcoholics. Growing up in that household was torturous—Steven was beaten by his father for the least infraction while his mother stood by helplessly. She offered him a maudlin "love" when she could: he remembers so many afternoons after school coming home to find her at the kitchen table, with her cup of tea (laced with bourbon), in tears. She would smother him with hugs and kisses and commiserate with him about his terrible father, her terrible husband. It was the closest thing to love Steven ever got, and it was preferable to the brutal beatings Daddy gave him.

Once, when his father came home drunker than usual and took a swing at Steven because he was a "fuckin' pansy wimp," Steven did the unthinkable. He swung back. He can still feel the impact of his fist on his father's jaw and see how his father seemed to crumple not only from the force of the blow but from the audacity of it. "It was like he lost all his spirit for a moment," Steven said. "It was terrifying." His father fell back onto the couch—Steven had hit him hard—and glared at him with what Steven says was "unimaginable hate." He then hissed at him to get out of the house and never come back.

Steven walked the streets of his hometown all night—it was late November, cold, windy, and he had no idea what to do or where to go. He rubbed the sore knuckles of his hand and cried into the wind, wishing he'd never been born, wishing he could somehow get the courage to do away with himself. He remembers huddling for a little warmth in the bushes of the town park until morning. He waited until he knew his father would be out of the house, then went home, expecting to gather up some clothes and take off. But when his mother saw him, she got up from the kitchen table, where she'd already begun her tea, and ran hysterically into his arms, pleading with him to stay—her "commiseration" had reached a new pitch. She promised everything would be better. Steven's father hadn't even *remembered* last night, she said. She promised to see a lawyer "first thing"—well, maybe the next day—get a divorce, and take Steven away from all this. Steven, all of sixteen, looked at his pleading mother, who was offering him all he'd ever known of love, and decided to stay. He almost wanted his father to come home. He almost wanted to take another swing at him. Despair was turning into anger. He wasn't going to take it anymore. . . .

I've given you this scenario because it gives some understanding of the compulsion from which Steven is only now beginning to recover. Brutalized his whole young life by his father, he had finally discovered the "joy" of seeing what it was to brutalize someone back. In fact, once Steven had taken that swing at his father, his father never again hit him. But that one punch had been so terrifying, as well as so satisfying, that it set Steven up for a craving for violence that has tortured him ever since.

The phenomenon of "eroticized rage" is hugely common in gay men and especially, from what I've seen, in compulsive gay men. It doesn't, I think, take a brilliant psychiatrist to point out why: when you feel brutalized by the world, as so many of us did, even if we didn't have as violent a father as Steven's, one clear way to "absorb" that brutalization—to psychically conquer it—is to sexualize it. Certainly this is what Steven did. Steven's sexual fantasies centered around sadomasochism. He preferred being the top, but with some men—he couldn't exactly predict who, it was just some unconscious chemistry, he said—he would allow himself to be the bottom. It took years before Steven realized that he would allow himself to be beaten up by men who reminded him unconsciously (you guessed it) of his father. But, either way, it was the *beatings* that were sexually arousing. Steven had very effectively eroticized his rage.

Like every other man we've met so far, Steven's compulsion took over his life. At first he assumed a Jekyll/Hyde personality: businessman by day, black leather "terror" by night. Then he got a job at a gay leather store in a big city, allowing him to deliver over his life to fantasy. His alcoholic genes did not fail him: although he had promised himself he would never take a drink, given the messes his parents were, beer was as much a prop in s&m gay life as black boots, and he found himself giving in—and drinking a lot. Before long, he was getting smashed on a very regular basis—both drunk and beaten up. I won't give you a litany of how bad it got, but suffice it to say that Steven seemed to be meeting a lot more men who unconsciously reminded him of his father. One night, drunker than he ever remembered being, he decided to look for some trade in a tough trucker's bar—a decidedly straight bar. Steven said he sidled up to a dark-haired bear of a man, who was the image of his dad, and slapped him on the rump. The man got up and smashed his beer bottle over Steven's head—at least that's what they told him at the hospital the next day when he woke up from his stupor with twenty-five stitches in his scalp.

Steven discovered AA much the way Grant discovered OA: the hospital strongly suggested rehabilitation. AA took hold, the way Twelve Step programs took hold of the other men we've met. The door to recovery opened—a crack. Steven was amazed there was another way to approach life and look at his problems, but his sexual fixation wouldn't "go away" the way alcohol did. He still was besieged by his old fantasies. He would buy wrestling and boxing magazines, in addition to gay leather porn, work himself up to a frenzied lust, and go out to his old haunts, carefully sticking to cans of Coke rather than beer, but otherwise getting himself into the same old messes.

It was around this time that he met Michael.

Steven had been peripherally aware of Michael for a number of months at AA meetings. Michael was quiet, pale, boyish—not Steven's usual type, which ran to the swarthy and bearish—and whenever Michael shared, Steven had felt a strong identification. Nothing, from what he could make out, was similar in their lives or backgrounds—Michael had evidently come from "normal" midwestern parents, a quiet middle-class home, and good schooling. But the pain Michael talked about feeling—the isolation he said he still sometimes felt even in a roomful of other recovering gay men, the internalized homophobia and shame he still grappled with—tugged at Steven every time Michael spoke. Michael's difficulties most recently had centered on the long, painful demise of a good friend who had just died of AIDS. It was making Michael confront, he said, the fragility of his own life and the need to feel "purpose" in what he was doing.

These ideas tugged at Steven not because they were issues he was consciously dealing with but precisely because they were not: Steven was only half-conscious that his increasing unhappiness was connected to a feeling of purposelessness. Michael was pushing a button, nudging Steven toward the fuller awareness that he needed to look at his life in a different way. One evening, this need felt particularly acute. He'd gone home with some older man the night before, a man who had a very involved fantasy of being tied up and spoken to as a dog—with Steven kicking at the cur and cursing it. Suddenly Steven became aware of the guy's small studio apartment and its idiosyncratic, personal touches—the framed family photos, a stack of opera records, a stuffed bear on a chair, a historical romance paperback with a grocery receipt as a bookmark—and here was this man, tied up at his feet, whimpering. Steven was nearly felled by a feeling made up in equal parts of shame, disgust, depression, and disbelief. What the hell were they doing? *Why* were they doing it? For the first time in a long time—if not the first time ever (Steven had sometimes reached these moments of self-disgust before, but they'd passed quicker than this one promised to)—he wanted to get out, get *away*. He no longer wanted to act out this way.

The next day, sitting across the room from Michael at an AA meeting, listening to his quiet, articulate voice, identifying for some reason more deeply than usual with the pain and grief Michael was expressing about his dead friend, Steven felt a rush of warmth, a softening toward him that made Michael seem to be, somehow, the "answer." After the meeting Steven walked over to tell Michael how moved he was by what he had said. Michael colored; he was as shy as a sixteen-year-old. Steven felt an answering flood of wanting to protect him—and hold him. Electricity crackled between them, surprising them both.

Coffee led to dinner dates and dinner dates led to "going home" with each other. (Steven couldn't remember the last time he'd dated this way; Michael couldn't believe someone as hunky as Steven could possibly be interested in him.) They went to Michael's apartment. Steven's apartment was always a mess and there was so much pornography and sexual paraphernalia lying around. He didn't, for some reason, want Michael to know about his sexual fantasies. Michael was "different"—a man who, maybe, might be able to "normalize" him, bring him relief from what increasingly seemed to have become the sordid squalor of his own life. Michael, in turn, was overwhelmed by the attentions of this "great, dark man." Michael was so physically slight next to Steven that he kept feeling, as he later said, "as if there had been some mistake. Why would Steven want a little twerp like me? Steven could have had anyone he wanted!"

These attitudes set up the dynamics between them. It's common for there to be a seesaw effect in love—where one lover feels he gives more love than he's getting back, or vice versa. Compulsive gay men who get involved in relationships often feel that the seesaw takes them precariously high and low. Because our self-esteem is so rocky to begin with, we are tempted to see ourselves in wildly fluctuating ways, ways that swing between the most abased self-pity ("I'm a piece of shit—how could anyone love me?") to the most grandiose flights of superiority ("Why can't I find anyone I *deserve?* Why is everyone so stupid and unattractive?"). These swings rarely are verbalized in their extremes, but they underlie—it's clear to me from my own life and from my unscientific survey of other gay men—nearly all of our relationships with one another. We are so often in this powerful, painful tug-of-war of unconscious one-upmanship: either admitting "defeat" or greedily acknowledging we are on top.

Things get particularly nasty because of something even less acknowledged between us: our deeply inbred homophobia. Although it's clear from the "phobia" part of that word that it means *fear* of homosexuality, we sometimes slide into defining the word as *hatred,* since that's how homophobia so often manifests itself. But it *does* mean "fear," and it's important to remind ourselves that that's what is at the root. Gay compulsive men are so mistrustful of themselves as individuals that they're intimately (if not always consciously) acquainted with that fear on many levels. We've swallowed whole the homophobia fed us by society and let it erode our self-esteem to the vanishing point. We think the deep secret is that we are monsters—but the deeper secret seems to be that we feel as terrified and vulnerable as cornered animals.

What this all boils down to is simple. It's a *miracle* two gay men—especially if one or both are compulsive—can survive an evening with each other, much less a long-term relationship! That some of us manage not only to "survive" each other but learn to find love is a testament to heroic human adaptability. Steven and Michael were not, at first, aware of anything more than a growing feeling of unease. Steven had not quelled his violent sexual fantasies by pushing them away in the desperate attempt to "reform" himself through Michael. And Michael's rock-bottom view of himself as unworthy of anyone's love or attention was not, unfortunately, magically ameliorated even by the attentions of a man as hot as Steven. It's not that there wasn't something genuine—a real love—between them; all the electricity they first felt between each other wasn't just disease-attracting-disease. But, as they discovered, when, through the first months of their relationship, their old habitual cravings and self-views didn't automatically disappear, they needed to take a look, individually, at themselves. They needed to face *who they each were* before there could be the chance of offering anything consistent and healthy to each other.

It is such a gift for two men to be in "recovery" in Twelve Step programs *and* to be in a relationship. As bad as things get between them, there is always, eventually, a common source of comfort and wisdom to which they can return. Sometimes, in Steven and Michael's case, this simply meant spouting slogans at the tensest times—letting the slogans, in a way, take care of them. "I used to think they were a lot of Sunday school jargon—Twelve Step sayings like 'Easy Does It,' 'First Things First,' 'One Day at a Time.' Now they help to *ground* us," Steven says, "when things get rough. And things did get rough there for a while."

Steven increasingly felt "trapped" and "deprived" in his

relationship with Michael, and there was nothing vague about what he felt he was missing: "Sex. I felt I hadn't really had sexual release with anyone in so long. I loved Michael, but my fantasies just weren't being met. It began to gnaw at me so much, I had to do something about it." Michael had a Thursday night Al-Anon meeting he especially loved. At Steven's urging, Michael had started going to Al-Anon six months after hooking up with Steven. ("We need all the help we can get—don't forget we were *both* involved with drunks!") Steven took the opportunity of a free night to roam around his old neighborhood. He connected with an old trick and went back to his old apartment—replete with all the sexual toys he had renounced since meeting Michael. "I was pretty much living with Michael by this time," Steven said, "but I held on to my old place—telling myself it was still too early to commit totally and give it up, but really holding on to it in case I wanted to use it for sex. I never said that to myself in so many words, but that was my real motive. The sex was hot and I managed, after the first pang of guilt, to rationalize it away—I was just giving myself a needed outlet."

Unfortunately, this "outlet" quickly escalated. Steven began to live for his Thursday nights out, which soon, of course, weren't enough. He contrived reasons to get away from Michael during other times of the week; his sexual compulsion had now returned full force.

Despite a strong reflex to rationalize Steven's absences ("I really wanted to believe Steven's stories about having to do this or that errand, meet this or that friend"), Michael knew something else was going on. He also had known for some time that Steven's sexual needs weren't being met by him. Because sex had begun to turn into cuddling, Michael could tell that Steven's "need" for him had become less urgent. Of course, this just fed into his feelings of inadequacy. "I felt, in a negative way, sort of validated—as if he were finally waking up to what a twerp I was." Then Michael began, as he put it, "to wake up and smell the coffee." He had always known that Steven worked in a leather store, but had always rationalized it as being part of Steven's gay life. Steven was so upfront about being gay that of course he'd want to work in a gay business. But now Michael allowed himself to see something obvious: "Of course Steven wasn't really turned on to me. Look where he spent his day! In an s&m store. I felt like an ass," Michael said. "Here my lover was, working in an s&m leather shop, and it never really occurred to me until now that he was attracted by that scene. Sure, he'd made comments about stuff in his past, but I convinced myself it was over. Now I knew it wasn't."

When Steven's absences became too glaring to ignore, Michael decided to do something. He needed to bring things, somehow, to a head. One day Steven gave him some excuse about having to look at some new merchandise for the store that "this guy" could only show him on Tuesday night—the following night. Michael nodded without saying anything, his stomach clenching not only at the lie he knew Steven was telling him but also with self-hatred: he was sick at his decision to follow Steven, but knew he'd do it anyway. "The next night I watched him from the window," Michael said, "to see which direction he was going, then quickly went after him, staying a block behind." Where Steven led him was to the gay area of town—Michael wasn't surprised at that—but he was shocked to see Steven walk into a bar. They were both alcoholics. Why would Steven jeopardize himself like this? (But what better place to meet someone than in a bar? a small voice reminded him.) Michael did not go in after him—he waited across the street. And waited.

"I've never felt more like an *addict,*" Michael said. "My eyes were riveted to that bar's door. A bulldozer couldn't have budged me." He stood there, shivering in the early December chill and damp, a cold sweat on his brow, "hating myself for doing this and Steven for doing it to me." Michael finally was "rewarded" by seeing Steven walk out with a big, burly bearded guy in black leather. "I don't know if I was more relieved or hurt," Michael said. "Relieved to see proof of what I knew was going on and hurt, stomach-wrenchingly jealous, that I couldn't be the guy who turned Steven on. I felt such a strange combination of hatred, rage, and fear. Somehow I got up the courage to run across the street behind them. I tapped Steven on the arm and watched him turn around. It was like I'd pulled a plug: his whole *being* seemed to drain out of him as he looked into my eyes."

The game was up. Or at least, the game had come out in the open. I won't bring you through the tears and accusations and lashing out and abject apologies that Steven and Michael put themselves through after this and a number of other similar episodes. What I will say is what began to emerge for both of them: the necessity of owning up to what each was feeling and doing and the impossibility of continuing to lie to each other and to themselves, not because lying was morally reprehensible but because it was so clearly getting in the way of their growth and happiness. With each brutal slam into the "wall"—each brutal recognition that, although they weren't drinking anymore, they were still, fearfully, in the grip of other compulsions that they knew would have to lift before either of them could lay claim to being "sober"—Steven and Michael are slowly getting to the point where their diseases don't do the "talking" anymore.

When Michael said that he "felt, in a negative way, sort of validated" by discovering "proof" that he was the twerp he thought he was, he was saying something that resonates in every gay compulsive man I've ever met. We are so used to hating ourselves that, in a strange way, we don't feel comfortable *not* hating ourselves. We are strange flies: given a choice between vinegar and honey, we gravitate to the vinegar—we do, that is, as long as we are not putting energy into our recovery. What we may call "self-sabotage" is really, from another point of view, a desperate attempt to *protect* ourselves by staying with the known over the unknown, even when the known is misery.

Steven says that being in AA and Al-Anon throughout all of this has been a godsend. "We broke up for a while at one point, but I was just running away from Michael and from something in myself. I was doomed to re-create the same stuff again and again, Michael or no Michael, if I didn't learn ways to face, and tolerate, myself. Working my program almost wouldn't *let* me lie to myself. That's the magic of it. As you hear so often in meetings, the program works *you*, you don't work *it*. If you let it, that is."

Getting through the thickets of denial and self-hatred that

gay compulsive men seem to face in love is, looked at in its entirety, a seemingly insurmountable task. Our hearts have been brutalized for so long by self-hatred, fear, and the erosion our compulsions cause. To repair them takes patience and trust. But, luckily, the essence of Twelve Step recovery lies in its manageability. Pay attention to right now and you'll be doing all you *can* do; don't expect that you can "solve" anything as complicated and terrifying as love overnight. We don't have to kick ourselves for not having acquired that patience and trust all at once.

I can't hope to have done more here than hint at the ways gay compulsive men have learned to face one another, heart to heart, human being to human being, head-on. Learning to do this means facing the ways in which many of us have compartmentalized sex and companionship, turning to lust over love. Sex is terrific, and it's homophobic to suggest that we should make it less a part of our lives than our hearts want us to make it. But "hearts" is the operative word. We, as compulsive gay men, need especially, it seems, to *integrate* sex with love if we're to stay "sober," in any sense of the word. As we've seen, it's not a process anyone can be expected to complete quickly or perfectly. But immediate strides can be made, so say my recovering friends, any time we want to make them. What it takes to begin making those strides is encapsulated in yet another Twelve Step acronym.

The road to any recovery seems to require "honesty, openness, and willingness": H-O-W. The Twelve Step message that you can develop and use these traits one moment at a time is a profoundly healing one. Perhaps it's by looking at the rewards of sticking to H-O-W in our own individual lives that we can teach ourselves what we need to know when we get involved with one another. You frequently hear in the program that "you're only as sick as your secrets." Test the truth of that by looking into yourself, and you usually begin to feel the flood of relief that comes from having been honest and open and *willing* not only to admit those secrets but also to understand what they can reveal to you about yourself. The simple answer to nurturing love among ourselves seems to be bound up, for so many recovering gay compulsive men, in this little acronym: H-O-W. It's a magic key into the soul, even if the room to which it gives access may be full of cobwebs and old baggage that have to be cleared out. But the program gives you ways to accomplish that too.

As always, we have more help to get through this process than most of us dream possible. And, at the risk of sounding heretical, not all of that help has to come from Twelve Step programs. Sustenance is available everywhere we look, once we become sensitive to its availability. You might even get some from your shrink—as we'll see in the next chapter.

Chapter Nine
Therapy: The Couch vs. the Steps

Many addicts have justifiable gripes against psychotherapy. "A lot of good it did me!" runs a typical complaint. "I was on the couch for twenty years and my shrink never once suggested that my problem just might be alcohol" (or sex addiction, or food addiction, or . . .). To be fair, there seems to be an increasing sophistication in psychotherapeutic ranks about treating addiction. Certainly most reputable therapists won't merely suggest AA or NA to alcoholics or drug addicts; in some cases, they *require* that their clients address their addictions as a prerequisite to therapy. The reason is simple: you can't get "better" if you're drunk or stoned. Therapy done while an addict is still drinking or drugging isn't therapy at all; it's expensive hand holding.

With sex, food, work, and other behavioral addictions that don't jeopardize the body and brain in quite the same ways as alcohol and drugs (notice I didn't say "as severely"—we all know we can destroy ourselves just as easily with, for example, sex and food compulsions as we can with booze or drugs), psychotherapists seem to be a little less adamant about suggesting a Twelve Step program. Any good therapist will tell you to do what works. But sometimes, because they may not know enough about them or may not believe that the Twelve Steps can work as well in behavioral (nonsubstance) addictions as they do in alcoholism or drug addiction, you won't always be told by a therapist to find the nearest SCA or CODA or Romantic Obsessives meeting. Indeed, as we've seen, dealing with addictions that require modification rather than eradication of behavior means changes in perspective (you can't give up food the way you can give up booze), so it's perhaps understandable if therapists don't automatically think of Twelve Step programs (other than AA and NA) as "supplemental" therapy.

Of course, to a recovering compulsive, all therapy *other* than Twelve Step programs is usually "supplemental." We find that we are able to recover because Twelve Step programs show us, right off, that we don't have to act out: the Twelve Step idea is that you act your way to good thinking, not the other way around. You *act* your way to recovery and only *then* figure out how to live (much psychoanalysis seems to proceed from the opposite premise). We must first *stop* the behavior that's the main cause of the mess in our lives.

Once we've done that, however, we've entered a new, wonderful (if sometimes baffling) realm. We've seen how much more there is to Twelve Step recovery than merely ceasing to act out (essential as that is). We're in for a store of serial revelations that are the direct result of living our lives according to Twelve Step principles. We see the joy that comes from connecting to other people in a fellowship—an astonishing feeling to people who, as individuals, never imagined they could be remotely like anybody else. We've seen how the general principles of honesty, openness, and willingness (H-O-W) can work in our lives. In short, we see how we can get the whole apparatus of our lives—an apparatus that our compulsions had once made grind to a dead halt—into working order, "merely" by adhering to the Twelve

Steps and attending Twelve Step meetings. Yet another deceptive simplicity you hear at meetings packs two solutions to all our problems in a neat sentence: "Don't act out, and go to meetings." Just heeding *that* is often enough to set in motion the domino effect of recovery.

But the world, as we've learned, is an abundant place. And, although there is a wonderful, healing "analysis" built into the Steps that places emphasis on inventory taking and responsibility, there are other kinds of analysis that can help us too. Many gay men turn to therapy even in the context of Twelve Step recovery: we are hungry people—as hungry for help and support and strength as we once were for our "drugs" of choice—and we are finding that help in some interesting places. It's productive to take a look at some of gay men's experiences with therapeutic alternatives and how they mesh with Twelve Step recovery from addiction because they give an abundant sense of the ways we can learn to grow. The world is wide open when we start to recover; there are infinite paths we can healthily choose to greater awareness and fulfillment. Many of us have found these paths rewarding as long as they spring off (and bring us back to) the main highway of our Twelve Step recovery. As any of us will tell you, we have nothing without our sobriety. All the gurus, shrinks, and psychic readers in the world can't help if you're too much in the throes of addiction to listen to them—as Don, in our next story, illustrates.

THERAPY "BEFORE" AND "AFTER"—MOORING THE MIND

"One of the biggest differences between going to a therapist 'before' and going to one 'after' is that he's not the only person I talk to now. Now my therapist is just one more alternative in my life—not the only one. But the biggest difference is that 'before' I hadn't any idea what I was doing, and 'after'—which means *today*—I actually feel I'm being helped."

Don says that when he still drank, "my life was a mess. It was such a complicated mess that I was sure it had complicated causes. I was entranced with the idea that I was 'unknowable' when I made the decision to seek out therapy. It wasn't just that I was in pain—which I guess I was, although the booze was zonking me out so regularly that I didn't allow myself to feel much of it—it was that I had this romantic idea that my complexity would dazzle my therapist. Maybe he'd do a breathless treatise on my fascinating personality. Maybe I'd stump him and he'd come to *me* for advice. I had a very grandiose view of what I could offer in therapy. All my wit and convoluted sensibilities and uncanny understandings—boy, I was sure I'd be a prize." Don confesses something else: "I knew enough about the psycho-analytic process to know I was supposed to transfer onto whomever the lucky analyst would be. That I'd probably even, in the course of therapy, fall in love with him. So my requirements for a therapist were that he be young, gay, male, and attractive. I figured if I was going to be doing all that transferring, it might as well be worthwhile. I was sure, even, that down the line we'd use that couch for something more than Freudian mind games."

Don found a therapist who fit the bill—in all senses. Because he had a low-paying job (one that he could do half blind, which he usually was after five or six vodka tonics at lunch), he couldn't afford high-priced Freudian analysts, and, anyway, he wanted someone to talk back to him, which he had heard Freudians didn't do. He found an attractive gay male therapist in a sliding-scale, gay mental-health clinic. "Just the ticket," Don says, "or so I hoped. I primed myself for our first meeting with a couple drinks—well, three drinks. I remember limiting myself to three because I knew that was the right number to loosen my tongue, relax me, allow me to be entertaining without quite slurring my words. So that's what I had before meeting Stan, my therapist, the first time. Stan," Dan continues, "was, however, a disappointment. He did *not* appear to be dazzled."

Stan quietly asked what agendas Don had in therapy, what he'd come to work on. Don answered enigmatically: "Everything—and nothing." (He thought he'd put on his existentialist beret; it would set the right tone of intellectual poignancy, he felt.) "I mean, what," Don says he asked, "is therapy anyway, Stan? An inquiry into the cosmos, exploiting me as the guinea pig and using my life as the crucible? An empirical study of what will probably turn out to be more *your* neuroses than mine, despite a clever doctor/patient set-up that would appear to suggest the reverse? I mean, really, Stan, what are we both here to do? Exchange a little hot air for some predetermined idea of 'mental health'? What mind games do *you* want to play Stan? What kind of white rat would you like me to be?" Don prattled on insensibly for most of his first session, feeling "brilliant" but making, he now knows, empty noise. "What struck me about Stan was that he sat there listening to me so calmly, making only the barest comment: the odd, interspersed 'Really?' or 'Hmm, why do you say that?' It was maddening. I finally told him it was obvious he didn't understand me and that we should probably call it quits, unless he wanted to have sex with me or something. I said I'd oblige him that way as long as he paid me, not the

other way around." Stan seemed to take this in stride and suggested that they talk about it the following week. He also
asked Don if he felt he had a drinking problem. "I remember
being appalled at his audacity. 'Have I mentioned alcohol
even once?' I asked incredulously, knowing that, apart from a
brief reference to the 'wine dark sea' when I dragged in
Homer for what even I realized was an infelicitous analogy, I
hadn't mentioned booze once. 'No,' Stan told me, 'but you
smell like a still.'"

Therapy did not, Don said, "bode well." But he decided to
come back the next week anyway. He had his medicinal dose
of three drinks before going, but he sucked on several breath
mints during the cab ride over to Stan's office so he wouldn't
be vulnerable to "attack" the way he was the last time.
Smelled "like a still" rankled, and Stan's tone of voice when
he said it—quiet, matter-of-fact, simply reporting the
news—had echoed in Don's mind the whole week. How dare
he? Don kept exclaiming to himself. Scented with pepper-
mint, he felt invulnerable and ready to dazzle Stan—for real
this time. But all of his pompous inanities burst like bubbles:
"Stan, I decided, was a hard nut to crack. He said, at the end
of the second session, that it might be a good idea to come
sober the following week. That maybe I should come without having had anything to drink for us to work together. I
smelled like a toothpaste factory—a commercial for Certs!
He thought I'd been *drinking!* 'I beg your pardon,' I said to him
as icily as I could, 'but these remarks about drinking are tire-
some and rude. Not to mention completely uncalled for.'
'Still,' Stan said, unmoved, 'think about coming here next
week sober.'"

Now *this* rankled Don all week. He was tempted not to go
back at all. But he didn't want to give Stan the upper hand.

He'd go and tell Stan what he thought about his impertinence. And, all right, he would forgo the drinks he usually had, but he would take some Valium instead. Don said, "Since I'd taken enough Valium to tranquilize a medium-size horse, I felt very loose, to put it mildly." Thus, stoked up, "or down," Don went through his third session, which he vaguely remembers sounded like a sixties hippie rap. Quoting John Lennon about going with the flow, Don then asked Stan why he got into the therapy business anyway, when he could have become something *useful,* like, he didn't know, a sheep farmer or something. . . .

The upshot of Don's early experience in therapy is pretty clear from these descriptions: he wasn't getting any. The weeks went on, and every time Stan suggested that Don might want to look into AA or perhaps NA (Don was astounded. Was the guy a mind reader? How could he tell when he'd taken pills?), Don reacted angrily or would sink into long fits of silent withdrawal. It's not that painful or even potentially helpful material didn't come up, but it came up, Don says, not only "at random" but as if it were in a surreal drug dream, which was pretty much what was happening. "I couldn't remember anything I'd said from one week to the next. Some resentments would hang on, but they'd usually be about how I could never get Stan to respond the way I wanted him to. He never told me he thought I was a genius, which I was trying to make him believe. I started to resent him." Don sometimes wouldn't show for a session, then apologetically show up with a check the next day, or he'd show up at the appointed hour, hand over his check with a flourish, and announce to Stan that this was what he was "*really* after, the money, wasn't it?" Then he would turn his back melodramatically and stomp away—in great indignation—to a bar.

Finally, Stan gave Don an ultimatum. Either he join AA or NA or they'd have to cease their work together. "Work!" Don spat at Stan, "you call this *work*? All you do is sit around while I spill out my guts, and now you tell me I have to go to some Romper Room group therapy before I can have the privilege of paying to spill my guts out to you again? *Please!*" ("God, I was an asshole," Don says today.)

Don did, in fact, go to AA. He hated it. He resented the hell out of what he felt were "Norman Vincent Peale-isms" and the self-evident happiness of so many of the people he saw. For the first couple of meetings, he left early and went straight to a bar. He was beginning to resent the hell out of everything. His life was, he had to admit, on a downward slide. It was—okay, he'd admit it—unmanageable. But it had nothing to do with alcohol except, perhaps, peripherally. "Abusing" alcohol might have been a symptom of something strange and dark and convoluted in him, but it certainly wasn't the cause of anything. What was beginning to hurt was that this "strange and dark and convoluted" self he'd once thought was so "glamorous" was now starting to make him physically sick. He was starting to hate himself. He had dreams about Stan, nightmares really, where Stan would stand up suddenly and walk away into a fog, and Don would call out to him. Once, Don dreamed he was in bed with Stan, but when he reached out to hold him, Stan had evanesced— disappeared into a mist. Don was miserable "for real" these days, and at first he continued to blame it on the "lousy therapist" he'd spent so much money on. Then he blamed it on the lousy vodka he'd had the night before. (If only he'd stuck to the top-shelf brand!) Then he started to blame it on himself. He was always a shit, anyway. "I mean, of course Stan would tell me to get lost! Who would want *me* around?"

It was in this mood of self-pity and psychic sickness that Don went to AA once again—he'd felt defeated enough now to give himself over to this bunch of loonies. What did it really matter what he did? But, for the first time, he really listened to what people were saying. They sounded a little less like Stepford Wives. They were talking about their pain— pain that wasn't so different, after all, from his own. The help offered by the program began to seep in. He was, without quite realizing it, "hooked." Nothing else in his life had worked, so he'd give this a try.

It's several years later, and Don has gone back into therapy—again to Stan. After a few false starts in AA, he's now committed to sobriety, and the world, he says, "couldn't be more different. My sessions with Stan gained meaning almost immediately, since AA was enabling me to be receptive in ways I never thought I was capable of before." The first difference Don told us he'd felt between "before" and "after" was particularly vivid now: Stan wasn't the *only* alternative in his life. "It's not that he became less important—he gives me something nobody else does, and the work I do with him is unique to us, and I cherish it. But I don't feel as if the only place where I can be honest is in his little office. I don't feel like I have to live my life in secret, storing up all the sordid details until I get to the next session with Stan. Now every moment of my life offers me an invitation to be honest and open and to 'work' on myself—thanks to the program. I can share what I learn in therapy at meetings and vice versa. Each brand of therapy feeds the other."

It's not always so easy to make a fluid transition between therapies. One friend of mine who's battling his food compulsions and sexual compulsions in Twelve Step programs had a difficult time, at first, reconciling Twelve Steps with his experience in one-on-one conventional therapy. "I don't know why, but as soon as my head hit the couch, I started to doubt everything I was learning in Twelve Step programs— I started to get cynical. I guess my expectations about therapy were getting in my way. I thought of my therapist as this judge sitting over me, chalking up this 'higher power' stuff as some deeply rooted desire for the 'father I never had.' It's hard to talk about the spiritual component—or at least it was for me. I always felt I had to explain to my therapist that my growing sense of 'God' wasn't a cover-up for some neurotic unmet need. Whenever I felt I had to explain the intangibles of Twelve Step recovery, I was sunk. 'Science' had to win out."

This friend of mine, as he submitted more deeply to the process he was undergoing with his therapist, began to realize he was projecting his own doubts and fears about Twelve Step recovery onto his therapist, and now the two alternatives he's exploring for psychic health don't seem to be as much in conflict. "I sort of let God do the analyzing in Twelve Step programs—I let my therapist do it in my sessions with him. Neither tells me much direct information, but somehow I've grown to feel they're not at odds with each other!"

THERAPY—AND PROGRAM—JUNKIES

The wonderful probing instinct that seems to run rampant in gay compulsive men can, as you're surely aware, either from your own experience or from the experience of others you know, sometimes backfires. It does seem to be true that we make the bump-in-the-rug connection especially quickly and allow it to propel us into various programs and therapies that we hope will mesh. But sometimes we can become addicted to therapy-going and therapy-doing in ways that don't ultimately help us very much. It's very common for this to happen *before* we end up in Twelve Step programs. Sometimes it seems impossible to find pre-Twelve Step people who *didn't* undergo est and Gestalt, group therapies of alarming configurations, and Eastern religious cults. We are a group highly sensitive to our hunger for something, anything, that works. I wish I could report that this mad scramble—or what turns out to be both too much and not enough help—stops when we turn to AA or NA or OA or DA or SCA or ACOA or any of the other As, but that's not always the case.

Witness Martin, a self-professed therapy junkie. "Before I caught on to Twelve Step groups, which, believe me, I needed, I was a pothead (by the time I was fifteen), and I had grabbed at any food, substance, or creature I thought would take me out of myself for most of my life. I went the whole sixties and seventies mind-expansion route. There wasn't anything I didn't do, from bowing before my own personal Buddhist shrine—I'd cleared out one of the two rooms in my apartment and made it into a temple at one point—to all the group therapies and trendy movements you've ever heard of. I remember rising in the ranks of Est to the point where I'd give the introductory talks to people curious about the program. It's a wonder they didn't all leave. I was supposed to be so inspiring that they'd all, en masse, plunk down their money for the Est experience. When very few did, I almost had a nervous breakdown, right in front of them. I pleaded with them to sign up. I called them stupid. I cried, 'Don't you see what a wondrous experience Est has been for me?' How could they possibly pass it up? How could they do this to me?

Boy, Werner Erhard couldn't have had a nightmare worse than me—I single-handedly made sure that at least two hundred people never signed up for Est!" Martin's group joining and hysteria had deep roots. "I was the fat, ugly kid in school. The only attention I could ever get was by joining chorus and band and the student council and every school club you've ever heard of. Join it, and then do my best to run it. My list of extracurricular activities went on for paragraphs." When Martin went to college, group joining began, if anything, to increase: "When I found uppers and pot, I found a way to be 'cool' and 'hyper' at the same time. I had enormous bursts of energy: I'd organize war protests and sit-ins and direct avant-garde theater, all virtually at the same time." What all this furious activity was blocking out was his terrible loneliness— the feeling that he was an entirely different species from anyone else. He felt desperately separate.

Martin's use of drugs escalated, and he landed, more than once, on the flight deck of various mental institutions. During one of his stays, he was encouraged to join an in-house NA meeting. The experience changed Martin's life in ways that are now familiar to us: he was able, through the Twelve Steps, to accept his powerlessness over the many substances to which he'd gotten himself addicted and to start living a drug-free life. But what wasn't cured was his group-joining compulsion. In fact, now he had a whole new arena in which to act out that compulsion. When he got out of the mental hospital, he threw himself full force into "program"—OA, NA, AA, CODA, and SCA—getting sponsors in each and a few sponsees as well. He began chairing meetings and qualifying whenever he could. His entire life was taken up with "program." He did freelance word-processing, which he squeezed into his highly programmed life so that he could support himself, but he worked as little as possible. Martin's friends told him later that they felt tremendous pity for what he was obviously putting himself through. It was a little frightening to see someone taking on the full garb of Twelve Steps and, yet, somehow missing something central. It's true Martin wasn't acting out—at least not for the first year of reentry into the civilian world after his last hospital stay. But even that, as you'll see, couldn't last.

Martin remembers the night he "picked up" again. "I got on a bus to go to a meeting I was supposed to chair—an NA meeting that I didn't really like, but they needed a chairman, so naturally my hand shot up. It's not that it was a bad meeting—no Twelve Step meeting is bad—it's just that I didn't know any of the people there very well. They must have been the last NA people in town I hadn't met! And I felt the usual burden of having to prove myself. God, when I think back to that time, that's really what I was always trying to do: prove myself and get accepted. Anyway, the bus broke down. There was no way I could make the meeting on time, because buses didn't run very often on this route and the next one would have been too late. I was tearing my hair out. What was I going to do? I thought of trying to hitch—but that was against the law. Then I realized where the bus had left me off. Right in the old drug neighborhood where I used to buy my stuff. I can't explain what happened—it was like my anxiety caused me to go into overload, and something suddenly snapped, shut down. I made the decision right then and there to get high. No remorse, no feeling at all. I knew I had to get high and that was it. Nothing could have stopped me."

Martin found his old barbiturate contact and bought a night's supply. He remembers that long gone but still famil-iar easing down into oblivion. It swept him away, down to numbness, just as he'd wanted it to do. But he remembers, before nodding out, feeling a kind of distant sadness, a blackness he was moving closer and closer to, that void he'd been able to escape for so long until now. . . . Martin turned into a pillhead again, started drinking again, stuffing himself with food again—it all came back. His sudden absence was very conspicuous since he'd "infiltrated" so many Twelve Step groups in town. He would sneak into his apartment, let the phone ring and ring or take it off the hook—and isolate. All his furious group joining had ceased, and what was left in its wake was a huge *absence*—not just of "therapy" but, Martin said, "of *self*. It became very clear that I could no longer keep away the void. All those attempts to 'get better' were feeble little stabs of effort that were doomed to fail. They couldn't cover up how isolated I felt, how empty."

Finally, a small coalition of Twelve Step people camped out on Martin's stoop, knowing Martin was holed up in his apartment and that he'd have to emerge some time. Hours went by and Martin didn't appear. Replacements took over so that there was a kind of twenty-four-hour watch, which Martin couldn't have escaped if he'd tried. Eventually, a stumbling figure appeared at the door and tried to get down the stairs. It was about midnight, Martin remembers. "I remember thinking, who are all these people on the stoop? I wondered if they were dangerous. I almost welcomed the thought. Maybe they'd do me in. That would be a nice end to things. I was so doped up I was almost ready to provoke them into mugging me. But then one of them called out my name. And they all rose up. I was scared. I knew these people from someplace. Who were they? One reached out his arms as if to hug me. I remember recoiling—what was he trying to do? Suddenly I didn't like the idea of being mugged after all.

I told them to go away. But they came closer. I remember screaming. It was so dark, and I couldn't see who they were. Then I saw my NA sponsor's face in the streetlight. 'It's okay,' he said. I was so doped up, I couldn't speak. But I could cry— boy, did I discover I could cry. They all came in and held me while I sobbed. I've never felt anything like it." Even now, Martin says, he can call up that night and feel the unconditional love—the unthinking embrace.

Martin said, "I once saw a bunch of monkeys on a man-made mountain in a zoo. There were three little babies of varying sizes—small, smaller, and tiny. All three were sitting in a quiet little group on a ledge in front of a small hole in the rock. Suddenly, with no provocation I could see, the littlest monkey was screaming his head off! He was having a *breakdown*. He turned away from the other monkeys and howled into the dark hole in the rock behind him. What happened next was amazing, and instantaneous. The two other babies simply, quickly, wrapped their arms around their howling little brother. A larger monkey—their mother?—leapt down and wrapped them all in her arms. It was so . . . matter-of-fact. Like, 'of course that's what needs to be done.' There was no thought. It was just a reflex action. A being needed to be taken care of and so you took care of it. That was it. That was the kind of love I suddenly saw was available to me. That's what they all did for me when I came 'howling' down the stairs late that night."

Nothing Martin had done—or allowed to be done to him—had ever really touched his loneliness before that night. What he began to realize is that he was overloading on service in the programs out of a desperate need to fill a void in him; he was acting out of fear, not out of the loving urge to help anyone else. Whenever Martin needs to remind himself that he, too, is lovable, he thinks of his dark night when people who loved him helped him—and of the monkeys. "And that's often," he says. "I need to be reminded every day of my life." He's begun going to a therapist whom he uses as a kind of monitor—someone to check reality with on a weekly basis, a reality he also "checks" by staying in frequent, not *obsessive,* contact with his sponsors. "I realize I was trying to turn my sponsors into therapists, and that's not what they are. They're recovering addicts, just like me, who are willing to share their experience, strength, and hope with me in a personal way. But they're not there to psychoanalyze me or to do any of the work *I* have to do for myself. I feel like I can let them be. I don't have to keep phoning them, shoving myself down their throats every minute of the day, much as I know they're always there when I *do* need them. Therapy has helped me sort this out a little. It's relieved the pressure. That unconditional love I've so craved is available in a variety of forms, and it won't go away. That's the most amazing realization. I can always go back for more. It won't run out. I was always afraid that help would run out. Now I know that help—that love—is infinite."

Help—and love—*are* infinite. This is what I learn every day of my life now that I turn to dependable sources of love and help every day of my life. Gay compulsive men are, from what I can make out, especially sensitive to "alternative" approaches to healing: the affirmations we learn from Louise Hay, the wisdom we've amassed from Joseph Campbell's work in myths, the road more and more of us are traveling via M. Scott Peck—these are only a few of the well-known thinkers and spiritual guides to whom some of us have turned to supplement the essential work we continue to do in Twelve Step programs. Not everyone is equally helped by the same guides. (One friend of mine scorns Louise Hay's affirmations as coercive and manipulative; another swears by her and listens to her tapes every day.) But the fact is we are actively seeking remedies—remedies to help us grow on the path already set out for us by the Twelve Step process. It's clear to me that we haven't forsaken our therapists, either. The psychoanalytic process they afford now seems, if anything, strengthened and improved by our involvement in Twelve Step recovery. The first reason is the most obvious: we are mentally *present* for therapy during recovery from compulsion in ways we simply can't be when we are not. But we are helped, by the Twelve Step route to recovery, in deeper and subtler, by participating in therapy too. As we recover, we learn to participate more in all areas of life. We learn to "show up," first in body, then in mind, and finally—through no special will of our own, but rather, it would seem, from an organic process set in motion by attending Twelve Step meetings and "working our programs"—*spiritually.*

The root of any true recovery is spiritual. And while I'm offering a discussion of that root as a final chapter, it's really what we've been talking about from page one.

Chapter Ten
The "S" Word

The "S" word? No, it's not sex. Or even sobriety. It's "spirituality." The ways in which we learn that our recovery from compulsion is spiritual are as various and surprising as each of us is; the universal truth seems to be, however, that the *strength* we draw on to recover is not only our own. Whatever way we visualize the source of that strength, whether we call it "God" or "Higher Power" or "the people in Twelve Step meetings" or any of the terms religions give us to define it, the effect on us seems to be, ultimately, the same: we feel plugged into something larger than ourselves. The big surprise, to me, is how different living a spiritual life is from what I imagined in the dark days of my drinking, drugging, uncontrolled promiscuous sex, and food cramming. You do not need a wimple to be spiritually plugged in. You do not have to kneel uncomfortably in cold stone buildings and spout arcane language to be spiritual. Spirituality has nothing to do with Protestant stiff upper lips, Jewish guilt, or Catholic *mea culpas*. It has to do with something far simpler, far less intimidating, far more personal, far more practical.

Spirituality, stripped of its incense-laden connotations, turns out to be a most useful trait. Developing spiritual resources means developing the ability to tolerate anything life hands you. If it's a blessing that we never know what life will hand us until it's happening, a greater blessing seems to be that God never hands us anything we can't handle. Let's leave, for a moment, discussions about the use of the word "God" and turn, rather, to the proof of this claim—a proof that is offered to each of us in each of our lives every day, but most dramatically during what we are told is a Big Moment.

Like dealing with death.

I was with my brother for the last two weeks of his life—before he died of AIDS. His lover and I nursed him in ways that may not have astonished his lover (who had been taking care of my brother for a good year and a half before this, and had gone to hell and back numerous times before these last days), but they certainly astonished me. If anyone had told me what was ahead of me before I got on the plane to go to him, if anyone had given me a list of what was going to happen, the kind of caretaking that would be required, the pain of seeing his physical self deteriorate moment by moment before our eyes, the pain of looking into his baffled face, baffled at the strange bodily demise he seemed sentenced to undergo—if anyone had told me what it would be like to wipe his ass, dispose of his urine, keep track of his medicine, help to change his sheets and his clothes, and tentatively (because his modesty was so great to the end, his shame at the physical indignity into which this disease had plunged him was so great, it had to be tentatively) reach out to hold his hand when we were through wrestling him into a more "comfortable" position or through cleaning him up—if anyone had told me this beforehand, my response would have been succinct: "You got the wrong man for this job." There was no way I could have dealt with all this—no way I could have taken the pain—no way I could have watched anyone, least of all someone I loved as much as I loved my brother, "die." That I ended up doing all this is a miracle, a miracle for which very little credit is due me.

My brother was a troubled, impatient, joyous, witty, moody, empathetic, intelligent, and profoundly spiritual man. These are all traits he knew he had, even if modesty and self-doubt would have kept him (most of the time!) from admitting the "positive" ones. But his spirituality was something palpable, especially near the end of his life. He hated his disease—he hated how it made him look, how boring the relentless decline of it was, how it sapped his energy. He went through some very bitter times, lashing out at anyone and everyone at the worst moments, railing at what was his complete impotence over what had attacked his physical being. But as this destruction waged in his body and sometimes his mind, something else was dislodged—visible at first only in glimpses, then slowly, pulled out of him like a hand from a worn glove. He began, through some process known only to him—although, I believe, potentially knowable to the rest of us—to emerge spiritually in ways that not only eased the inevitable passage he faced but also eased us as we watched him face it. I said before that spirituality was a *useful* trait. I learned that in the last days of my brother's life. As his body failed him, and talking became such a great effort that he all but abandoned it, he spoke through his eyes. When I touched him—when his lover came in to touch him, greet him, tell him volubly and cheerfully about the world "outside"—my brother's great, large eyes would focus for a moment and let us read his response. What was that response? "Thank you. I love you." It didn't matter what we said, toward the end, or what we did. Even when he cried out involuntarily because moving him (as we had to do when we changed him) tore at his bedsores, when we let him sink back into his pillows and get the strength to focus his eyes for another moment, there it was again. "Thank you. I love you."

It's amazing the energy he gave us. Sometimes I think we did what we had to do to take care of him solely on the strength of those simple, wordless messages. He was stripped, finally, to the light in his eyes, and though that light was, at the end, only intermittent, it provided the most abundant fuel I have ever known or could ever hope to know.

I always used to think that "pass on" was a euphemism for "die." Watching my brother make that passage now convinces me it's far more accurate than "die," which implies cessation. I saw no cessation. I saw a moving-on, not only a leave-taking but a going-to. By this time his eyes no longer focused—except, perhaps, inwardly: his energy was imploding, softening and severing the ties, the final ties, that kept the "hand" in the "glove." But he had given us so much love by the end that we were buoyant enough to be there for him. It was a question, almost, of physics—we were available to him because he had given us precisely the right amount of the right kind of energy to be there. His spirituality had pulled all of us through. Being present at my brother's leave-taking was the greatest privilege I've ever known. It was also an incalculable gift. He took away my fear of death. I now know in my heart, mind, and soul that there is nothing to be afraid of when we face this passage.

Other gay compulsive men I've spoken to who have lost lovers, friends, and brothers through the plague of AIDS echo me on this point—even if they weren't there at the moment of passing. Often, just having been there during the last months and weeks of "softening and severing" makes the knowledge of "passage" seem simple and true. All the bull

sessions that we may have had (often drunk, if we were alcoholic) about the Meaning of God and Life now seem childlike
and distant. We have had this great fact shoved into our faces
by AIDS, and the fact seems to be that "death" isn't at all what
we feared it would be. Instantaneously, for many of us, we've
achieved a new perspective about our lives: now we're more
concerned about what our "tasks" may be, what "purpose"
we may be here to fulfill before we make that passage ourselves. The deaths of our friends and lovers open, for many of
us, yet another door to the vast realm we've already glimpsed
in recovering from compulsion—the infinite realm of sobriety. We get further—and now, if we need it, irrefutable—
proof that we are not alone, that there is not only a God but
that He/She/It *is in all of us* and truly *connects* all of us. The proof
of this has happened in our own hearts, our own experience.

I mention my brother's passing not for sympathy. If it comes
to that, I offer mine to you as readily as I know you offer yours
to me: who hasn't been through this crisis in direct, painful,
inescapable ways? But the miracle I spoke of earlier is what I'd
like to focus on. The fact that I could be there for my brother
and his lover—the fact that his inchoate love could reach
me—all are due to my sobriety. Not only alcoholic sobriety,
but what I hope is a growing emotional sobriety. I hear so
many tales from all manner of addicts that make clear how
desperately we once turned to our addictions to get us away
from moments like the ones I faced with my brother—like
the ones you have faced in your own life. To awaken from that
fear, to find the strength to face and get through life, is a miracle for any compulsive person. AIDS is such a challenge to all
of us, not least to gay compulsive men who need to face that
some of their compulsions have made them more likely to
have contracted AIDS. HIV-positive recovering addicts are a

special inspiration, as are gay men "in program" who live with and die from this disease. Sobriety, to all of our amazement, has prepared us even for this! And the means of preparation are spiritual. We have learned to turn our lives over to a spiritual force that is both larger than us and part of us. We get better by connecting to this source consciously. The Twelve Steps themselves culminate in this firm assertion. The Twelfth Step begins, "Having had a spiritual awakening as the result of these Steps. . . ." The steps leaves us in no doubt about the fact that a "spiritual awakening" is ours for, if not the asking, then the earning. Perhaps both.

It is so frightening, now, to see the lack of this consciousness in gay compulsive men around me who are not in recovery. I don't walk into many bars these days, but sometimes I do, either to meet a friend or out of a perverse and usually misguided attempt to see how the other half lives. I am always amazed by the crush and noise and desperation—the smoke and hardness and barely disguised fear. I'm probably projecting much of this from memories of my own desperation, when I turned to these gay emporia for *everything*—but I'm not projecting all of it. Not long ago, on one of my infrequent raids into the gay wilderness, I stopped into a bar for a club soda. A short, drunk, disheveled man grinned broadly at me and gestured widely around the room with his glass: "Life's a bitch, isn't it?" I smiled back and said nothing, then turned to get the hell out of there. Life was *not* a bitch for me anymore, although it could very easily turn back into one if I ever decided to trade my club soda for what I used to tell bartenders to pour into my glass.

All addictions operate on us in the same way with regard to spirituality: they drain it. They sever us from trusting anything but the substances and/or behavior offered as panacea.

I once "Twelve Stepped" (program talk for helped another person to get sober) a friend some years ago, a Twelve Stepping which has not, alas, so far stuck. He was moved to tears by the stories of people at the meetings—so moved that he was able, for a while, to accept that he was "one of them." He stopped drinking and he stopped acting out sexually. Both of these activities he'd engaged in to excess, the "excess" you've read about in this book. But he never raised his hand to speak in meetings. He never took phone numbers. When I wasn't around to take him to meetings, he didn't go. Because his lover was a heavy drinker, he was surrounded by booze (and its discontents) at home. It was virtually inevitable that he would pick up another drink—which he did. His old behavior flooded back within a week.

But he hasn't been the same man since. There's a greater sadness in him now. He knows what it's like to be free of compulsion, and drinking and acting out sexually are tainted now—different, even less satisfying than they were when he'd given them up before. We share the same summer house, and I remember a group of us out on the deck, my friend sunning himself and gabbling on, drink in hand, to a friend of his he'd invited out from the city. I was reading, but more than half aware of the wandering, unmoored mind of my drunken housemate. How sad it was to listen to him! The same, endlessly repeated stories about sexual conquests, movie stars met, sledgehammered "witticisms" that he desperately meant to be sophisticated and cutting but which all fell flat. His moods changed like random colors in a kaleidoscope—at one moment laughing, at the next belligerent, at the next maudlin, the next dead serious ("Now let's *really* talk, okay? Can we *talk?*"), the next giggling at the unwitting imitation he'd just done of Joan Rivers, but throughout all of this, badly pleading for attention. He tugged, sometimes literally, at the bored friend at his side, badgering him with "Don't you agree?" and "You know what I'm talking about, don't you?" It was exhausting—enervating to watch and probably unspeakably enervating to participate in. My heart went out to the bored friend, but it wrenched for my drunken friend. He was like a balloon detached from its string, blowing anywhere, everywhere, nowhere. How I hope his dissatisfaction will continue to get worse until he wakes up to his own powerlessness over addiction! A seed was planted in the days he stopped acting out, and I know that seed never dies, even when it's trampled on the way he's trampling on it now.

I think of my friend as an unmoored spirit. Mooring his spirit wouldn't, however, mean trapping it or keeping it from growing. Mooring your spirit *allows* it to grow. If we can be likened to plants, the analogy is especially clear: we need a place for roots to go down before we can grow up. Addictions are hatchets, forever severing us from any chance of throwing down those roots. Spirituality is in this way profoundly practical. It's not some ethereal, otherworldly, transcendent state to which we can only distantly aspire. It's what gets us through breakfast. Work. Love. The supermarket. Calls to mother. Loneliness. Moments of triumph. Depression. Joy. Boredom. Twelve Step recovery has enabled so many of us to tap into this "river"—to get unending sustenance from spiritual resources. Acquiring that sustenance sometimes comes through waiting for someone to finish a sentence. Sometimes it comes from restraining anger when we know that blurting something out will be hurtful. Sometimes it comes from acting quickly, decisively, and positively even when we're afraid of the outcome—even when we'd rather not get involved.

Spiritual sustenance is built into the Twelve Steps. We cannot follow the Steps without becoming spiritually nourished.

So much more can be said about every aspect of recovery that we've explored. The Twelve Steps have been dealt with here as a kind of pastiche. Although I said early on that I didn't plan to offer an exegesis of the Steps because wiser people than I had already done so, I do feel the lack of a straightforward reading of those Steps. You probably do too, especially if you're not already familiar with them. But if I've exasperated you, perhaps that may work to your advantage. Perhaps you'll be exasperated enough to want to explore those Steps yourself—to vault yourself into the recovery you've read about here. If there are missing links in this book—pieces of the puzzle you find glaringly absent—my dearest hope is that those lacunae will challenge you to fill them in with your own life and experience and quest. You can't, in any event, "get" recovery from any book. As you've seen, you have to build it into your own life, or, at least, take the first steps toward building it into your own life. In this way, you can become open to the infinite help available to you.

I hope you're open to one realization above all: we deserve to love and accept even the most abased parts of ourselves—even the "you" that was on his knees in a men's room or passed out in a gutter. Love's fraternal twin is forgiveness. I once heard in a meeting the following Judgment Day scenario, and it's one I've taken into my heart and ask you to take into yours: "When you appear before God on that day, He won't ask you what you did right and what you did wrong. He'll ask only one question:

'Did you know how much I loved you?'"

Please realize that you are loved.

RESOURCES

DRUG AND ALCOHOL ADDICTION

Alcoholics Anonymous (The Big Book). 3d ed. New York: Alcoholics Anonymous World Services, Inc., 1976.

B., Hamilton. *Getting Started in AA.* Center City, Minn.: Hazelden, 1995.

Johnson, Vernon E. *I'll Quit Tomorrow: A Practical Guide to Alcoholism Treatment.* San Francisco: HarperSanFrancisco, 1990.

Narcotics Anonymous. 5th ed. Van Nuys, Calif.: Narcotics Anonymous World Service Office, Inc. 1988.

Twelve Steps and Twelve Traditions. New York: Alcoholics Anonymous World Services, Inc., 1981.

ADULT CHILDREN OF ALCOHOLICS, AL-ANON, AND CODEPENDENCY

Al-Anon Family Groups. New York: Al-Anon Family Groups Headquarters, Inc., 1984.

Beattie, Melody. *Beyond Codependency: And Getting Better All the Time.* Center City, Minn.: Hazelden, 1989.

——. *Codependent No More: How to Stop Controlling Others and Start Caring for Yourself.* Center City, Minn.: Hazelden, 1992.

In All Our Affairs: Making Crises Work for You. New York: Al-Anon Family Groups Headquarters, Inc., 1990.

Mellody, Pia. *Facing Codependence: What It Is, Where It Comes From, How It Sabotages Our Lives.* San Francisco: HarperSanFrancisco, 1989.

Woititz, Janet Geringer. *Adult Children of Alcoholics.* Deerfield Beach, Fla.: Health Communications, 1990.

SEX AND LOVE ADDICTION

Carnes, Patrick. *Contrary to Love: Helping the Sexual Addict.* Center City, Minn.: Hazelden, 1989.

———. *Don't Call It Love: Recovery from Sexual Addiction.* New York: Bantam, 1992.

———. *Out of the Shadows: Understanding Sexual Addiction.* Center City, Minn.: Hazelden, 1992.

———. *Sexual Anorexia: Overcoming Sexual Self-Hatred.* Center City, Minn.: Hazelden, 1997.

Hope and Recovery: A Twelve Step Guide for Healing from Compulsive Sexual Behavior. Center City, Minn.: Hazelden, 1994.

Mellody, Pia. *Facing Love Addiction: Giving Yourself the Power to Change the Way You Love.* San Francisco: HarperSanFrancisco, 1992.

Sex and Love Addicts Anonymous. Boston: The Augustine Fellowship, Sex and Love Addicts Anonymous, Fellowship-Wide Services, 1986.

Sexaholics Anonymous. Nashville: Sexaholics Anonymous, 1989.

Schaeffer, Brenda. *Is It Love or Is It Addiction?* Center City, Minn.: Hazelden, 1997.

FOOD ADDICTION

Overeaters Anonymous. Rio Rancho, N.M.: Overeaters Anonymous, Inc., 1980.

R., Helene. *Take It Off and Keep It Off: Based on the Successful Methods of Overeaters Anonymous.* Chicago: Contemporary Books, 1989.

The Twelve Steps and Twelve Traditions of Overeaters Anonymous. Rio Rancho, N.M.: Overeaters Anonymous, Inc., 1993.

Westin, Jeane Eddy. *The Thin Books.* Center City, Minn.: Hazelden, 1996.

GENERAL RECOVERY AND BACKGROUND

B., Hamilton. *Twelve Step Sponsorship: How It Works.* Center City, Minn.: Hazelden, 1996.

Carnes, Patrick. *A Gentle Path through the Twelve Steps.* Center City, Minn.: Hazleden, 1993.

Kominars, Sheppard B., and Kathryn D. Kominars. *Accepting Ourselves and Others: A Journey into Recovery from Addictive and Compulsive Behaviors for Gays, Lesbians, and Bisexuals.* Center City, Minn.: Hazelden, 1996.

Kurtz, Ernest. *Not-God: A History of Alcoholics Anonymous.* Center City, Minn.: Hazelden, 1991

Larsen, Earnie. *Stage II Recovery: Life Beyond Addiction.* San Francisco: HarperSanFrancisco, 1985.

————. *Stage II Relationships: Love Beyond Addiction.* San Francisco: HarperSanFrancisco, 1987.

Z., Phillip. *A Skeptic's Guide to the Twelve Steps.* Center City, Minn.: Hazelden, 1991.

SPIRITUALITY AND RECOVERY

B., Mel. *New Wine: The Spiritual Roots of the Twelve Step Miracle.* Center City, Minn.: Hazelden, 1991.

Levine, Stephen. *A Gradual Awakening.* New York: Anchor Books, 1989.

Martin, John. *Blessed Are the Addicts: The Spiritual Side of Alcoholism, Addiction and Recovery.* New York: Villard, 1991.

ABOUT THE AUTHOR

Guy Kettelhack has written seven books on recovery. He is completing a master's degree in psychoanalysis and is an analyst-in-training at the Boston and New York Centers for Modern Psychoanalytic Studies. A graduate of Middlebury College, Kettelhack has also done graduate work in English literature at Bread Loaf School of English at Oxford University. He lives in New York City.

Hazelden Publishing and Education is a division of the Hazelden Foundation, a not-for-profit organization. Since 1949, Hazelden has been a leader in promoting the dignity and treatment of people afflicted with the disease of chemical dependency.

The mission of the foundation is to improve the quality of life for individuals, families, and communities by providing a national continuum of information, education, and recovery services that are widely accessible; to advance the field through research and training; and to improve our quality and effectiveness through continuous improvement and innovation.

Stemming from that, the mission of the publishing division is to provide quality information and support to people wherever they may be in their personal journey—from education and early intervention, through treatment and recovery, to personal and spiritual growth.

Although our treatment programs do not necessarily use everything Hazelden publishes, our bibliotherapeutic materials support our mission and the Twelve Step philosophy upon which it is based. We encourage your comments and feedback.

The headquarters of the Hazelden Foundation are in Center City, Minnesota. Additional treatment facilities are located in Chicago, Illinois; New York, New York; Plymouth, Minnesota; St. Paul, Minnesota; and West Palm Beach, Florida. At these sites, we provide a continuum of care for men and women of all ages. Our Plymouth facility is designed specifically for youth and families.

For more information on Hazelden, please call 1-800-257-7800. Or you may access our World Wide Web site on the Internet at http://www.hazelden.org.